THE GOOD PARTNER

Understand the things
you can change.
Let go of the things
you can't.

A
modern
approach
to
relationships

THE
GOOD
PARTNER

KAREN
NIMMO

HarperCollins*Publishers*

HarperCollins*Publishers*
Australia • Brazil • Canada • France • Germany • Holland • India
Italy • Japan • Mexico • New Zealand • Poland • Spain • Sweden
Switzerland • United Kingdom • United States of America

First published in 2022
This edition published in 2024
by HarperCollins*Publishers* (New Zealand) Limited
Unit D1, 63 Apollo Drive, Rosedale, Auckland 0632, New Zealand
harpercollins.co.nz

A catalogue record for this book is available from the National Library of New Zealand

ISBN 978 1 4607 6527 2 (paperback)
ISBN 978 1 7754 9221 4 (ebook)
ISBN 978 1 4607 4316 4 (international audiobook)

Cover design by Andy Warren, HarperCollins Design Studio
Illustrations by Megan van Staden
Typeset in Sabon LT Std by Kelli Lonergan

Printed and bound by CPI Group (UK) Ltd, Croydon, CR0 4YY

'After enlightenment, the laundry.'
                                    – Zen proverb

Contents

Introduction: Sex, then dishes

A woman I've just met tells me she's blissfully in love. Then she bursts into tears.

Freya, who's in her mid-30s, has booked into therapy to talk about her relationship with Quinn. They've been together for a year. He wants her to move in with him, but she's hesitant about making The Big Commitment. *What if it doesn't work out? What if he's not the guy for me? What if I waste more time on the wrong one?*

I wait, expecting a roll call of his negative traits – that he's emotionally shut-down, a heavy drinker, a gaslighter, ogles other women, doesn't pick up his dirty socks – but she heads in the opposite direction.

'He's perfect,' she says, twisting aggressively at the friendship ring he's given her. 'He's easily the best partner I've ever had. He's kind, caring, smart, funny … we have such a great time together.'

She shuffles in her seat. I know there's a *But* coming. 'But,' she says, on cue. 'I can't get my head around this whole commitment thing. Will it be the same deal, night after night, forever? Sex, then dishes.'

I can't help myself. I lean in conspiratorially. I watch her curious expression. 'You've got it,' I say, 'apart from one thing.'

I pause, a therapist's tool for creating suspense. 'There are a lot more dishes than sex.' Actually, what I'm really thinking is, *there's a lot more everything than sex*, but I keep that to myself.

Freya swipes a tissue from the box, dabs her eyes and grins. 'Do you think we need to come in for a session together before we do this?'

'You're here now,' I say. 'Why don't we begin with you?'

***

Like Freya, people often raise their relationship problems in individual sessions, when they're on their own. It's like they grab the chance to speak freely and test the relationship waters – without upsetting, worrying or getting into a fight with their partner, as often happens in couples therapy.

It's a good idea. Not because couples therapy or counselling doesn't work – it can and does – but because there's another way to improve your relationships. And that is to analyse yourself. To delve into who you are as a person and why you roll the way you do, and focus on what *you* bring to the kitchen table, rather than what your partner is (or isn't) bringing. After all, you are the only person you can ever hope to fully understand. And you're certainly the only one you can be sure of changing.

Without question, our relationships test us. Show me a couple who floats through life without niggles, struggles and a slammed door or two – sometimes a whole lot more – and I'll have seen a miracle. Either that, or they're lying. But being equipped to create and maintain good relationships matters, because they're such key contributors to our wellbeing and, when they don't go well, our misery. This matters now more than ever, in a world where divorce and separation rates are climbing, families are more diverse, and we're all struggling with the pressures and uncertainty of 21st-century life.

The good news is great relationships are made, not born. True, some relationships are not built to last – and some people not built to stay in them – but it's worth learning skills to help you play the game as well as you can.

The tougher news is that love is hard to pin down. There's no blueprint for the complexity of intimate human connection. But, as I've talked about love and relationships with hundreds of people over the years, seven core themes have emerged, which are central to all relationships. I call them The Seven Pillars of Love: *Trust. Communication. Conflict skills. Intimacy. Load-sharing. Play. Kindness.* These pillars don't stand in isolation. There's a significant overlap between them but, together, they form the foundation of a healthy, loving relationship – and offer guidance as to being a good partner within one.

These pillars are underpinned by the therapeutic models I use in my work. All therapists have their favourite models – or methods of working – but we're united in saying that whatever we use should work in our clients' best interests. My approach is fluid: I like to draw threads from all sorts of places to match the needs and personalities of my clients. Having said that, I'd like to acknowledge four key influences in my work, and this book.

1. **Cognitive behavioural therapy (CBT)** This helps you to identify, challenge and change unhelpful thoughts, beliefs, behaviours and situations. It's a brief, action-oriented, problem-solving model, which can be used broadly as well as for diagnosed mental health issues.
2. **Acceptance and commitment therapy (ACT)** A values-based therapy that combines self-acceptance with mindfulness skills. ACT is about being present with life's challenges (and difficult feelings), and moving towards behaviour that aligns with your values.

3. **Positive psychology** This branch of psychology is concerned with happiness and wellbeing. It's not about positivity at the expense of processing honest feelings. Instead, it encourages reflection on the factors that most contribute to a well-lived and fulfilling life.

4. **Meaning therapy** The roots of this therapy are in psychiatrist and Holocaust survivor Viktor Frankl's Logotherapy. It focuses on finding meaning in life; the human capacity to make life worth living, in spite of challenges, suffering and limitations.

***

This book is a do-it-yourself guide for anyone who wants to do better in love – in the relationships you're already in or those you aspire to have. It's not about bringing out the toolkit and trying to 'fix' yourself. Nor is it about pointing the finger at your partner. This book is about figuring out who *you* are – or become – in relationships, understanding your vulnerabilities, triggers, reactions and behaviours. It's about equipping yourself with tools to help you cope with challenges and iron out your difficulties, as you work towards being content and at ease in your relationships, your own unique version of a good partner.

I've drawn heavily on my work with people of all ages and relationship stages when researching this book. While theory and research must underpin therapeutic work, we can learn so much from the experiences of others, from their stories, through looking at the world through their lens. I've done some of my best learning from the couch, because people are endlessly surprising. Just when you think you've heard it all, you'll hear a story that sends you skidding back into the rookie zone and hot-dialling a supervisor or colleague for help.

The examples I've used are true but, in the interests of ethics and confidentiality, I've taken care to omit and/or disguise all identifying details. This means some of the people who appear in this book are a compilation of traits. So, if you think you recognise yourself – or anyone you know – please dismiss it as a remarkable coincidence.

Finally, relationship advice has traditionally focused on exclusive partnerships between two people. While this is what you'll find in my examples, it's important to note that modern relationships are diverse. They require an approach that is inclusive and accepting of people's differing values, cultures, orientations, needs, beliefs and desires. In other words, there are no fixed rules, as long as it's legal and consensual (every time).

The Good Partner is built on the premise that the better you understand yourself, the better you'll relate to another person. It requires some soul-searching – and some honest self-diagnosis. So if you're in a relationship, don't let your partner read this book over your shoulder. Your flaws are your business – there's no need to rush to share them!

On that note, let's begin with a test to gauge your 'status' as a partner.

PART I

FROM THERE TO HERE

The Good Partner Test

Are you a good partner?

Most people are a little uncertain how to answer that question. Many of us will say, 'Hmmm, I'm okay on a good day.' But we all know only too well how our relationships look on a bad day, and no-one's hurrying to open that door.

We also often don't know for sure what a good partner is. When our relationships are going well, we don't stop doing the dishes and try to figure out why. Just as people don't usually rock up to therapy when life is going well, we don't tend to pull apart what's working in our relationships. We roll with the 'Why fix what ain't broke?' philosophy, and just get on with it. It's only when our relationships crack or break down that we want to know where they (or we) went wrong.

When you've been struggling in a relationship, you can lose your radar on what it means to be (and have) a good partner, or even what a healthy relationship looks like. Or maybe you've never known because you haven't had the right modelling? Or you've had a string of difficult relationships – partners with 'issues' – that has messed with your idea of healthy love?

The truth is, there's no definitive 'yes' or 'no' answer to what makes a good partner. The question is too broad; it's like asking someone if they eat healthily. They'd say something like: 'Well, I'm pretty good most of the time, but I do have a thing for cheese-burgers and fries.' You need to help people unpack what, where, when, why and how they eat – and the best way to do that is to ask specific questions.

It's the same in relationships. People are complex; while we may share certain traits, none of us fits neatly into boxes. There's no such thing as a perfect partner and you should bolt from anyone who says they are. We all have our quirks and foibles, our good and bad days, our strengths and vulnerabilities, our inner demons and – hopefully – angels.

But in order to 'do' relationships well, we have to understand what a healthy relationship is – as well as have a clear idea of what it means to be a good partner. Here's a test to help you figure it out. The questions are in no particular order but in various ways each of the seven pillars of love is covered.

The Good Partner Test

Answer 'Yes', 'Could do better' or 'No' to the following:

- **I freely admit when I am wrong.** I can apologise fully, without being prompted or having an agenda. I show my remorse in both my words and actions.
- **I have my own independent interests and friendships, and I make time for them.** I am happy for my partner to do the same – and encourage them to do so.
- **I'm fun to be with.** I can be upbeat, have a laugh and share a dumb in-joke with my partner. I am not perpetually gloomy. (You get a leave pass here if you are depressed or struggling with mental illness, but you

don't get one if you are not actively working on your difficulties. It's not fair on partners or families to leave your recovery to chance.)

- **I'm not a Drama Queen or King.** I don't overreact (too often). I am consistently able to manage my emotional reactions. If my partner were looking over my shoulder while I do this test, they would agree with me.

- **I agree with my partner over the time we each spend on our devices and recreational activities** (including alcohol, drugs, porn, gaming, sex, social media and spending money). If we don't agree, I'm working on my part of it!

- **My go-to conflict resolution style is reasonable.** I usually settle an argument in a fair and healthy way. (Note: Storming out, giving the silent treatment, vanishing into your emotional cave for two days, withholding sex and picking over issues endlessly aren't healthy strategies.)

- **I (mostly) keep our relationship in the present.** I don't repeatedly bring up old wounds or past conflicts. I don't compare my partner with someone from my past.

- **I make an effort, physically, emotionally and socially.** I do chores. I do my share with the kids (if we have them). I talk. I listen. I attend important events. I'm nice to my partner's key people. I suggest things. I don't wait for my partner to come up with all the domestic and social ideas, or 'organise' me and, if I do, I don't complain about my busy schedule.

- **I share the emotional load with my partner.** I give at least as much as I take. I talk to them about their worries. I ask how I could be more supportive (and I try to do it).

- **I'm dependable.** I do what I say I'll do, I'll be where I say I am, and I'm a reliable sounding board for my partner when they are struggling.

- **I'm generous.** With my time, energy and attention. I give at least as much to the relationship as I get.
- **I support my partner's hopes and dreams, but not to the point of martyrdom.** I know I deserve support for mine, too.
- **My relationship standards are fair.** I don't expect my partner to be a super-hero or heroine, and/or to meet all my needs. I'm able to function well independently.
- **I treat and speak to my partner with the same respect I show friends, people at work or in other settings.** I treat my partner as I like to be treated.
- **My partner always feels safe with me.** Physically, sexually and emotionally.
- **I don't play games.** I don't manipulate, abuse, gaslight, control or criticise my partner excessively. (Note: This is a trick question. People who do these things won't admit to them anyway, and they'd never take a 'stupid' relationship quiz.)

Results

Mostly 'Yes'

It's a hard job being the perfect partner, but you sound like you're close. This test was designed for humans, however. Are you sure you're not a robot? And why are you reading this book?

I'm kidding. Relationships are more complex than this, and we all have our limitations. While there's no such thing as perfect, you're getting close. You have all the elements of love in place and you're contributing to them. You are generous with your time, energy and spirit. You are complimentary, kind and supportive. When you disagree, you can step back and apologise genuinely. You can overlook minor annoyances in your partner for the greater good of the relationship. Sure, you have your moments, but not too many of them. Best of all, you're up for doing even better. Well done.

Mostly 'Could do better'

You're doing well as a partner but, like almost everyone, there's room for improvement. We all have communication struggles, arguments and battles over whose turn it is to do the vacuuming. We're all vulnerable to distraction, and the temptations of technology have amped up the problem: we could solve a lot of difficulties if we just put our phones away and paid more attention to our partners. But that's a challenge when a 24/7 source of entertainment is just a click away.

Aiming to be a good or better partner is great, but it can be hard to know where to begin. This test may have highlighted areas where you could improve – it's a useful starting point and you'll find lots of ideas in the pages ahead.

Mostly 'No'

Hmmm. You're definitely not a robot, are you? At least you're honest, even if you do have (a lot of) work to do!

Seriously, not many people who are inclined to take a test like this will come in with a lot of 'No' answers. Just by getting involved, you've shown you're an invested partner – and that's a good thing.

If you've spotted some glaring faults in yourself, don't be alarmed. You've just got a generous margin for improvement, and a starting point for quietly going to work on them.

Finally, whatever your score, it's time to put aside the labels. We're all a little of everything. Just think of your answers as knowledge you need to embark on your journey.

***

In Part II, we'll explore each of the pillars in turn: what they mean, how they play out and the struggles – cracks if you like – that accompany them. Finally, we'll look at how we can work on them. For those already content in their relationships (most of the time, at least), there's plenty of good oil you can apply to your own situation. Because, even when a relationship is in great shape, there's work to do. There's no such thing as lying back with a cocktail in the great deckchair of love, saying: *Look at me. Look at us. We've got this.* Complacency has a nasty habit of biting us where it hurts.

Before we dive into the pillars, let's take a look at how you landed here, on Planet Relationship. What, and who, has made you who you are in love? This means taking a brief tour back in time. Strap yourself in.

Planet Relationship:
How did you land here?

Roll back to your first serious relationship. You showed up with your Love Learner-plates on, driven by hormones and a desire – maybe even a need – to be liked and accepted, while not fully understanding what was going on.

If you were lucky, you got through it without too much pain. If you weren't, you'll recall the hurt, questions and recovery time. To most of us, relationships are hugely confusing. Sure, a few chosen 14-year-olds lock eyes across a crowded classroom and stay happily together for life. But, for the rest of us, love is a mystery tour of lust, infatuation, anxiety, screw-ups, questionable choices and pretty average sex. It takes a long time to understand the game, and even those who play it well are loath to say they've nailed it.

It's no wonder, when you think about it. There's no formal training for how to be in a relationship. When starting out, most people are armed only with what they've absorbed from not-necessarily-reliable sources: their parents and families, friends, gossip, the internet or TV shows, and movies.

Schools offer help with career choices; work experience; health and sex education; online safety; and even how to budget, drive and cook, but where's the class called Relationships 101? Where's the lesson on what it means to be someone's partner – and what to look for when choosing one? Where's the help with what a healthy relationship looks like – and what it's definitely not? Where's the rulebook for dealbreakers? How do you learn to express your desires and needs, settle a fight, manage your own emotions, know what's fair and what's not? How do you learn to be (or live) with someone else?

See what I mean? That's why when you land on Planet Relationship it can feel alien to you, an unfamiliar and bewildering place. There's no fancy GPS to guide you. All you have is a rough chart cobbled together from your past experiences. Your personalised chart of the heart. Let's take a look at how it formed.

Little you: Your history

Psychology has a reputation for wallowing around in the past. We owe that stereotype to the original masters of the craft, whose patients lay on chaise longues, as they were asked soft-voiced questions about their relationships with their mothers.

While many of us still have couches, modern psychological therapy has come a long way since then. Largely, therapeutic models are built, or adapted, to fit the needs of clients and focus on what will improve their lives right now.

That's not to say the past doesn't matter, however; because it does. And we need to go there, at least a little bit, because where we've come from holds mighty clues to the people we are now. It can also be the source of beliefs and behaviours that get in the way of who we want to be in the future.

Freya, who we met in the opening pages, was struggling to commit to her partner, Quinn. She admitted she was almost looking for a way out of a potentially great relationship. The reasons why were buried in her past.

When we unpacked her story, she found her difficulties had less to do with Quinn, and more to do with her own history of loss that had caused her great pain. Both Freya's parents had died in a car accident when she was 12, and then her beloved older (and only) sister, who had helped Freya through her teen years, had died of cancer when she was only in her 20s. So Freya was well acquainted with loss, and it made her terrified of getting close to anyone, in case she was hurt again.

The soundtrack of her life had become: *If I love them, I'll lose them.* She couldn't bear to go there again.

Her history had caused her to sabotage good relationships: she'd been aware of what she was doing but couldn't seem to help it. But this time, she was up for doing things differently. 'I can't lose Quinn. I can't let my past wreck my future with him.'

Like Freya, people often want to know if their relationship struggles can be tracked back to their past. *Has my family history disadvantaged me emotionally? Have I missed out on vital emotional lessons? Have I been left incapable of loving someone appropriately?*

These are good questions. And the answers – like anything in psychology – come in shades of grey.

There's no doubt the past shapes and informs us; it sets us up for who we become. And the ways in which our families function, interact and handle emotional issues can influence our adult relationships, sometimes significantly. Research tells us so – and every psychologist has seen the evidence.

So we need to look broadly at what shapes our relationships, remembering that no matter where we've started, it's possible to do things well, better or even brilliantly.

Your love bucket: Why you love the way you do

The way you love is influenced by many factors. These are connected in varying degrees and your biology and personality characteristics also weave through the mix. This unique combination makes up the contents of what I call your 'love bucket': the traits, beliefs and behaviours you bring to love. Some people begin their love lives with a bucketful of rich experiences, which gives them a head-start in relationships. Others have fewer or difficult experiences in their buckets, which can make navigating love harder or more confusing.

It's important to remember that when it comes to the human condition, *nothing* is set in stone. The contents of your bucket don't guarantee a particular outcome. As is the mantra of psychology, everyone is capable of change, of doing things differently, *if* they commit to it. Psychologists see two things over and over that make us sure of this:

- Negative early experiences don't necessarily lead to bad relationship outcomes. In fact, they may work in the opposite direction because you're determined to remedy the past, create something different from what you've seen or experienced.
- Loving parents and a great start in life don't mean relationships will be easy for you. It may even make it more bewildering when things go wrong, or if your relationship is not what you thought it would be.

Whatever your early experiences, it's helpful to explore them because they affect your belief systems around relationships and your expectations of what should happen, how you should behave, what your partner should be like and what you deserve.

As you read on, keep your history – the contents of your love bucket – in mind. But hold on to the knowledge that no matter who you are and where you've come from, you can make changes and improvements. You can do things differently if you're up for it.

Let's take a look at the key influences on how you love. Under each one, I've added questions to help you dig into your own experiences. If it helps, you can make notes or mark questions as areas you want to explore.

Your early attachments and environments

Attachment refers to the bonds you form with your early caregivers, based on the studies of psychiatrist/psychologist John Bowlby and psychologist Mary Ainsworth with children. Their research, as well as later studies, suggests that having secure, loving early attachments provides a solid platform for adult relationships. Equally, insecure or unpredictable bonds can lead to struggles later in life, including difficulties with relationships and intimacy.

Early environments are also hugely influential. They include cultural factors, the position and role/responsibilities you have in your family, the atmosphere (including conflict/violence) at home, and any issues your parents have (for example, their alcohol and drug use, and their physical and mental health). Any experience of abuse – physical, sexual or emotional – is an important consideration.

Questions to explore:

- *Were my early attachments close and loving? Warm? Supportive? Cold and distant? Disrupted? Negligent? Unpredictable?*
- *Was a primary caregiver struggling with their own issues?*
- *Were there birthing or health difficulties that may have influenced my early care?*
- *Was my emotional health or safety compromised? How?*
- *How did this beginning affect my expectations in relationships?*
- *What beliefs about love were set up for me?*

Your personal traits and factors

These include your biology/genetics – the personality traits you're born with – and those you develop, or that exaggerate, over time. While our personalities do morph and change with time and circumstance, people arrive in the world with different traits or characteristics – anyone with more than one child will vouch for that.

These factors also include developmental, health or disability issues, which can influence how you enter and maintain relationships.

Questions to explore:

- *What are my best traits?*
- *Am I/was I able to bring these to my relationship? Why or why not?*
- *What can't I change versus what could I change?*
- *What do I struggle with?*
- *What would I like to improve on?*

Your emotional inheritance

You bring an emotional 'story' into your relationships. This story can range from family experiences – such as loss, abandonment, parental divorce or conflict – to the emotional 'education' you received at home or picked up through various experiences. Some people refer to emotional inheritance as 'baggage'. It's not a word I like to use, because baggage is generally seen as negative. You can also carry forward positive emotional characteristics.

Questions to explore:

- *Did I feel loved? Was I told so, and/or did I feel loved and valued? Did my parents or caregivers listen to me?*
- *Were my parents/caregivers able to express and convey their own emotions? How did they express their feelings?*

- *Who was I closest to growing up and what was my relationship with them like?*
- *Did I get accurate and supportive feedback on my emotional responses to challenge, triumph, disappointment, rejection and hurt?*

Your relationship history

This is all about your personal experiences of intimate relationships and the way you feel about them; what you've learned and how it has helped or wounded you. It includes the modelling by your parents and significant adults (and how you experienced those things), the number and type of partners you've had (and the way you've been treated by them), the ratio of failed:successful relationships and the beliefs about love and trust this has set up in you.

Questions to explore:

- *Which of my intimate relationships influenced me the most?*
- *How was I treated by my partner?*
- *How did I treat them? How did it end – and why? Was it loving and ended naturally? Or hopeless – neither of us knew what we were doing? Or emotionally abusive, physically violent or just the right person at the wrong time?*
- *What have my past relationships led me to believe about relationships, a particular gender or myself?*

The feedback you've received: Nasty or nice

Feedback you've had from family, peers, teachers and the world generally (e.g. comments, compliments, labels, critiques and/ or bullying) has a heavy influence on how you see and perceive yourself. This feedback can be reflected in your relationships and how you function within them.

Questions to explore:

- *Was my feedback positive or negative? (Examples of negative feedback might include bullying, exclusion by friends or teachers, or comments on your body or looks.)*
- *What beliefs or labels might it have led to? (For example, I'm not attractive; I'm too overweight to ever get a partner; I'm smart; I'm sporty; I'm pretty.)*
- *What are three words I use to describe myself? Are they healthy and helpful – or not?*

Your current partner

Your partner (and everything they bring with them) can hugely affect your relationship style – your interactions, thoughts, habits and behaviours. For example, someone who is in a toxic relationship will be significantly impacted by their partner's behaviours. Equally, a healthy, secure partner can bring a positive influence.

Questions to explore:

- *Is my current relationship solid? Trusting? What one word would best describe it?*
- *What are our strengths together?*
- *What are our problems/areas to work on?*
- *What is my partner's best quality?*
- *What would they say is mine? Have we changed over time? Who has changed the most and why?*

There's one more influence in relationships too, one your past is not responsible for: Luck.

Luck

Luck or good timing or synchronicity – call it what you will. But we all know people who've blundered into relationships without much experience or knowledge, and it just worked out – even turned into a fairy tale.

Maybe they grew together over time? Maybe they were more compatible with their partner than it seemed on the surface? Maybe circumstances conspired to help out?

However it happened, they just got lucky – and I wish there was more luck to go around. If that's you, great, but it's still worth thinking about why, and giving yourself credit for your contribution, because even luck needs to be worked on.

***

Whatever your situation, know that you don't have to change your history for things to be okay. The silver bullet in improving relationships is to understand where we've come from, identify those things we can change and get better at – and let go of the things we can't.

Now you're aware of the contents of your 'bucket', you're ready to explore who you are in love, using the seven pillars as a guide. I've arranged the pillars in a sequence I might use in sessions with my clients. That said, there are no rules. Feel free to tap into them any way you like.

PART II

THE SEVEN PILLARS OF LOVE

Are you secure in love?

'As soon as you trust yourself, you will know how to live.'
– Johann Wolfgang von Goethe

Why does it matter? Trust means you can speak openly, confide in and feel safe together, physically, sexually and emotionally. It allows you to be vulnerable. Trust lets you breathe out and relax in a relationship: it frees you both to be yourselves. It also means you're not tempted to break into each other's phones.

***

When you want to explore who you are in love, trust is the place to start. People who are struggling in love don't usually roll up to their first therapy session and say, 'Please, help me with my trust issues.' They'll say they're feeling insecure, unhappy or disconnected in a relationship or that, in some way, they've been hurt. And those issues frequently have their origins in trust wounds.

Trust weaves through every aspect of our relationships. It's there in our choices; how we communicate, show vulnerability, have sex, share chores, fight, work, play, relax and treat each other. In short, it's the bright yellow signpost to the way we love.

We *all* have some degree of insecurity in our relationships. If you don't believe me, think of it like this: No-one is born in the perfect circumstances into the perfect family, has lived the perfect life, and turned into the perfect partner in the perfect relationship. These people might exist, but I haven't met any of them. I might not rush to either. Our fears, wounds and jagged edges are what make us unique, and fully human. Sure, some are luckier than others – and some are a whole lot unluckier – but we've all been let down; we've all got sensitivities and vulnerabilities. So I like to think that we're all on a sliding trust scale – it's where we sit, and how we got there, that makes the difference.

When we pare it down, there are two types of trust in relationships:

1. *The trust we have in a partner.*
2. *The trust we have in ourselves.*

Most people think being able to trust their partner is the bigger deal. That's understandable; no-one wants to be betrayed. But, while it matters hugely, we should remember that we can't control our partners' choices. We can't force them – or anyone – to treat us well; we can't take out a lifetime warranty against hurt and pain in love. Or anything, for that matter.

What we can do is work on building trust in ourselves, which is more psychologically helpful. Self-trust promotes security in love. It reduces doubt and worry, allows us to be vulnerable, helps us to rate ourselves as people and partners and to believe we're worthy of love. And, when our relationships crash and burn, it helps us to pick up the pieces and learn to love again.

We'll explore both types of trust and why they're important to being a good partner. But first, let's take a look at what can happen when trust issues collide. Here's Hana's story.

A tale of two trust issues: Hana's story

Hana, a professional woman in her late 40s, has come to therapy because she's looking for a relationship. After being divorced for 20 years, she says she's finally ready to get back in the game.

'You haven't been on a date since?' I ask, trying not to sound surprised.

She'd swept into my office, a blur of cream linen and gold jewellery, one of those effortlessly chic women who make you wish you'd taken more care with your own outfit that morning.

She shakes her head, but grins in a way that's almost a wink. 'Don't think I've been sitting at home, knitting all these years. I'm no virgin martyr. I'm just an expert at keeping men where I want them.' She pauses. 'I'm scared stiff of intimacy, even in my friendships, if I'm honest. I've come to see you because it's time I had – or at least tried to have – a real relationship.'

Hana described her marriage as 'beyond toxic' but her trust issues had a longer tail. Her father had been a work-obsessed, aggressive alcoholic. Unable to stand up to him, her mother retreated into the background, sending a passive message to her only daughter. 'I never knew what I was going to get when I got home. I didn't trust my dad not to be in one of his moods and I didn't trust my mum to protect me,' Hana said.

There was more. From the age of 8 to 11, she was sexually abused by a neighbour's son, who was a few years older. 'I had a crush on him,' she said, 'so I did everything he wanted me to do. I think I've only just acknowledged it to myself as abuse.'

Hana's experiences led her to not only mistrust others, but doubt her choices in love and her ability to be a good partner.

They had caused her to love in ways that would protect her from hurt. To erect a wall between herself and others – then try to form close bonds with them from behind it. In opening up about her struggle to form close relationships, however, Hana had taken the first step towards doing things differently.

What's trust got to do with it?

Stories of broken trust often fall under the sex, lies and secrets banner, probably because scandal makes the best gossip. But trust isn't always broken in *Shock, horror!* ways. It *can be* eaten away by a thousand tiny cuts, when you're repeatedly let down by someone you love and supposedly loves you. I once worked with a man who struggled for years with his wife's alcoholism. Again and again, she promised him that she'd get sober. Each time, he'd cling to that beat of hope but – every time – those plans would go up in a cloud of chardonnay fumes. In the end, his own mental health failed. And she kept drinking.

Having your trust broken can be life-defining. But people can, and do, recover to love fully, if they commit to taking steps to do so. I've seen both sides: People who have been almost frozen in time with the pain of betrayal, so they never give themselves a chance to live fully. But I've also seen people whose lives have improved dramatically because of broken trust; the change it forced on them and who they became because of it.

***

Delving into your trust issues takes courage. But, if you're up for it, ask yourself: Where am I at in my love life right now? Is there a problem? If so, what is it – specifically? What's maintaining it? How is it impacting me?

Take a moment to note down your answers – either on paper

or in your head. An unwritten rule of psychology is that before getting down to some heavy-duty self-analysis, you need to have a good grip on any problems. I'd go a step further. That is, if you don't get clear about what's wrong, you might as well invite trouble over for dinner and pour it a wine. You'll end up running around in circles.

Ironically, most people don't give trust in relationships much thought – until it's not there. We might thank our partners for making a meal or picking up the groceries, but we don't say 'Thank you for being trustworthy.' Which we probably should. Instead, we'll think: I can trust my partner, so all good – I don't need to worry. But I encourage everyone to think about trust, because it's so entwined with the other pillars, especially intimacy, communication and conflict.

The first task is to get a baseline measure of how (or how much) you trust. Use these scales to mark where you rate yourself right now. If you're not currently in a relationship, you can use the scales to reflect on how you felt with a previous partner. (Note: You might use them to remind yourself why you're no longer with them.) Or you can just use them to figure out what's important to you.

Here are some questions to guide your answers.

Do I trust my partner?

- ❏ Do I trust them to be open and honest with me?
- ❏ Do I trust them to make good choices when I'm not there?
- ❏ Do I feel safe to share my body, thoughts and feelings with them?
- ❏ Do their actions make me feel secure?
- ❏ Do they make me feel good about myself?
- ❏ Can I be fully vulnerable in front of them?

1 – 10
(Deeply suspicious...Highly trusting)

Do I trust myself?

- ❏ Am I open and honest with my partner?
- ❏ Do I treat my partner well – physically, sexually and emotionally?
- ❏ Do I make good choices when my partner's not present?
- ❏ Does my partner feel safe to share openly with me?
- ❏ Do I believe I'm an equal player in the relationship?
- ❏ Do I believe my partner is lucky to have me?

1 – 10
(Deeply insecure...Highly trusting)

If you have high levels (scoring 8 or more) of trust on both scales, that's great. Chances are your current relationship is stable, or you're happy with your status. But even if you're satisfied with your response, it's helpful to dip into your history to better understand where your thoughts/beliefs, emotions and behaviours about trust might have come from. To find out why things *are* working, so you can repeat them.

If you find yourself scoring on the downside of either or both scales, or you're unsure, this chapter will hold some answers for you. What matters most is whether any trust problems are holding you back in love, or preventing you from getting the most out of your relationships.

Here are the common ways that trust issues affect people. Check if any relate to you.

- You feel awkward getting close to someone intimately.
- You expect to be betrayed (part of you thinks it's inevitable).

- The idea of making an emotional commitment scares you.
- You're scared to let your guard down fully (so mostly, you don't).
- You either trust people easily or take ages to trust them (you worry you don't have a sound 'trust radar').
- You need a lot of contact with your partner to feel okay.
- You become clingy in a relationship when you're not usually like that.
- Your relationships and friendships are more superficial than you'd like them to be.
- You look for ways to get out of (or sabotage) a relationship when there's no real reason to do so.
- Even slight breaches of trust by a partner feel traumatic (e.g. they show up late when they're usually on time).
- You have very high standards for others.
- You tend to feel lonely or isolated, even within a committed relationship.
- You feel insecure with a partner, even when there's no need to be.
- In a relationship, you worry excessively about being left. Or outside a relationship, you worry about ever finding anyone.

Hana, my client, answered 'Yes' to nearly all of those statements. But many will relate to some of them. Anyone who's had their trust broken is naturally hypersensitive to having the wound re-opened with the prospect of more pain. And, when it recurs, they can have intense emotional reactions.

I worked with a woman who'd had a trauma-ridden childhood, but recovered admirably, settled into a relationship and had a family of her own. When she and her partner split by mutual agreement after 10 years, she coped well. But when he started a new relationship, she fell apart. It dragged her back into the turmoil of her past: tears, rage, panic attacks, anxiety and dark thoughts of revenge. She was mortified by her intense response, but it was understandable – even expected – given her history. When she understood this (and was reassured she wasn't going insane), she gave herself permission to feel these emotions without acting on them and to show herself some compassion. Slowly, she began to feel better.

Is your past holding you back?

Difficult life experiences – such as loss, abandonment, rejection and abuse – can lead us to view any potential partners, or people and the world generally, with suspicion. Lack of trust can make us do almost *anything* to avoid a repeat of those feelings, including pushing love away. And this has wider, and not necessarily healthy, implications for our lives.

This Trust Chain shows how trust issues develop.

```
            ┌─────────────────────┐
            │      BIOLOGY        │
            └─────────────────────┘
                      │
                      ▼
      ┌───────────────────────────────┐
      │           EARLY               │
      │   ENVIRONMENTS / PEOPLE       │
      └───────────────────────────────┘
                      │
                      ▼
      ┌───────────────────────────────┐
      │      LIFE EXPERIENCES         │
      └───────────────────────────────┘
                      │
                      ▼
      ┌───────────────────────────────┐
      │         FEEDBACK              │
      └───────────────────────────────┘
                      │
                      ▼
                  HOW
                  WE
                  TRUST
```

Our biology, parenting, early environments and life experiences lead us to develop a set of core, or deep, beliefs. These beliefs underpin who we are and affect our thoughts, emotions and behaviour. The feedback we receive from the world, and others, further sculpts our view of ourselves. If our core beliefs are negative, we're more likely to gravitate towards the messages (and people) that support those beliefs. That's what can keep us stuck, or lead us into unhealthy relationships. By understanding this chain, we can begin to challenge our old beliefs and move forward.

The Trust Chain can be broken in many ways. The tragic loss of a parent, early trauma and abuse are obvious examples. Here are some others I've heard from clients:

- My best friends in high school ganged up on me and shut me out.
- My parents were more interested in their work than me.
- I was bullied by kids at school.
- My brother was the golden child and got most of the attention.
- My sister had anorexia, so my parents had to focus on her.
- My parents' divorce left me with no-one to talk to.
- I never really knew my dad.
- My mum had mental health issues, so I had to be the parent.
- I only found out I was adopted when I was 18.
- I found out by accident that my uncle was my biological dad.
- My best friend dumped me for the new girl in class.
- My boyfriend persuaded me to 'sext' him graphic photos, then shared them with his friends.
- My first partner called me horrible names/abused me (there are many variations on this theme).

***

Trust exercise

Perhaps something on this list has resonated with your own experience? But whether they did, or didn't, consider what might have influenced your trust base. It's important to note that people suffer to varying degrees, depending on other factors such as their base resilience and network of support.

These are the key questions to ask:

- Who hurt me?
- Who let me down?
- Who did I love and lose?
- How might this have affected the way I love?
- How would I describe myself in a relationship?

Now, complete this sentence (writing down as many words as you can think of).

To me, loving someone means:
1. ....
2. ....
3. ....

Your answers are revealing: They will offer information as to why you might be resistant to, or feel insecure in, love. Or why you might rush into it too easily. Or both!

If you've had a tough experience, be gentle with yourself, especially if difficult feelings resurface. While we can't change the past, we can acknowledge and grieve for it. And we can, and should, show ourselves some compassion. We can also view it as contributing to who we are, and how we function, in relationships.

'Attaching' to others in love

Infant attachment is a topic in its own right because of its impact on how (and who) we come to love. Many studies have shown a link between early experiences with parents/caregivers and our adult relationships. That is, our approach to love is underpinned by a bias towards security, anxiety, avoidance or ambivalence – or various combinations.

Kids whose parents reliably respond to their physical *and* emotional needs have the greatest chance of developing a secure attachment style. A secure style indicates a higher likelihood of attaching healthily to romantic partners, just as kids who don't form secure bonds may later struggle in love. But *who* you attempt to attach to (and *their* attachment style) are also strong influences. Plenty of 'secure' people have found themselves in difficult relationships with unstable partners.

Different researchers favour different takes on attachment styles. Here's a brief summary of how these four styles might look in adult love.

Attachment styles in adult love

Secure
- Is open to trusting others.
- Rarely worries about being left by their partner/s.
- Feels comfortable with being vulnerable in relationships.
- Feels like a worthy person in their relationships.

Anxious
- Fears being rejected or left.
- Worries they aren't lovable.
- Needs a lot of reassurance in relationships.

- Tends to feel more invested in the relationship than they believe their partner to be.

Avoidant
- Feels stressed by the concept of intimacy.
- Resists emotional investment in their relationships.
- Struggles to share thoughts and feelings.
- Doesn't like to ask for help/support.

Disorganised
- Strongly fears rejection/abandonment.
- Lacks balance in relationships – tends to be 'all in' or 'all over'.
- Behaves unpredictably in relationships.
- Struggles to love in consistent ways.

Perhaps you recognised a tendency to one style? Or a mix? For example, it's possible to be both anxious and avoidant, and many people can be a little disorganised in love, depending on their circumstances and the relationship in which they find themselves. Obviously, secure attachment is preferable and disorganised attachment is the toughest place to come from – but everything can be worked on.

***

While it's helpful to explore your attachment style, it's not necessarily easy. In therapy, it can be hard to get to the roots of a person's early attachment, simply because one's memory doesn't stretch back that far. And asking your parents about their relationship with baby-you can be unproductive. Chances are, they were sleep-deprived and up to their neck in nappies, so their memories are unreliable. Or they default to the good times, or prompts from the baby photos.

Sometimes, the root of attachment difficulties is clear. One of my clients spent her first three years in a Romanian orphanage. Through painful discovery, she found her infant cries for food, discomfort and nurturing were never answered. She drew a link between that chronic neglect and her struggles as a young woman to trust or love anyone – and she was probably on point.

Often, however, we just don't know. Most parents start out with good intentions. But some give their kids a rocky start, for all sorts of reasons: drugs, alcohol, difficult birth experiences, post-natal depression/anxiety, other mental health issues, lack of money or social support, conflict within the relationship, or just their own limitations. The thing about parenting you don't, and can't, truly understand until you become a parent yourself is that no guidebook can EVER adequately cover all the scenarios, issues and emotions you will go through with your kids.

All of that means our understanding of relationships is a mashup of the messages we've picked up from home and life generally. As kids and adolescents, we work out what we must do to have our needs met, fit in, make friends, and be approved of and loved. Then we 'get on with it', in the best ways we can. It's not until we step onto Planet Relationship that our trust history quietly comes out to play and begins to shape who we are in love.

When you've been hurt, it's tempting to heap the blame on your parents, or the friend who dumped or bullied you in school, or your treacherous partner. After all, they probably deserved it. In the end, however, it matters less where the hurt came from and more about how it is impacting your relationships now – or those you want to create.

To improve or get the most from our relationships, we need to build trust in our partners, ourselves or – frequently – both.

#1 Trusting others: Who are they really?

The process of trusting another person kicks off from the moment we meet someone we're attracted to. Without even realising it, we're scanning for clues we can trust them. *Will you text when you say you will? Do you really look like your profile pic? Do you follow through on our plans? Do you genuinely like me? Can I count on you? Should I take a leap of faith?*

The trouble is, we're too dazzled by emotions and hormones in the early stages to give those questions our full attention. To be fair, relationships would never work if we all started out looking for the worst in each other.

A lot of clients have said that although they'd heard early warning bells, they brushed them aside, deciding it was too soon to tell and everyone deserves 'the benefit of the doubt'. One man said he could remember his new girlfriend's rage at a waiter when their meals took longer to come out than promised. 'It was weird; she was so angry. I remember thinking: "Whoa, cool down – you're way too mad over this," but I let it go. I didn't want to cause a scene. … And she was also damned hot – you know what I mean?' he smiled, sort of sadly.

I did. Sex is always a big drawcard. A decade later – divorced with three young kids – he was struggling to put his life and mental health back together, after spending years with a woman he could never rely on. 'She was all over the show,' he said, 'and it was absolutely bloody exhausting.'

Can I trust my partner?

Trust issues frequently surface in new relationships, but they also cause hurt and conflict inside established relationships, such as when one partner lets the other down, through either a betrayal or little things they do (or don't do), which then burgeon into big problems. These can lead us to doubt our choices: *Did I ever really know this person?*

It's impossible to know everything about someone at the start of a relationship. Even those people who we think we know may not turn out to be who they seem. People reveal themselves slowly, or they change with stress, circumstances and time. That's okay. Well, maybe not always okay, but it's something we have to live with. All we can do is arm ourselves as best we can for being with Someone Else.

To do this, there are two questions to consider:

1. *What tells me I can trust someone?*
2. *What does a healthy, trusting relationship look like to me?*

Let's look at each question. Then, you can use these as a guide for your own experiences.

What tells me I can trust someone?

At the outset, we're only seeing a snapshot of who a person is – and it's what they want us to see. The Big Reveal may come later. As you decide whether you're in or out, it's helpful to be aware of the positive signs.

I devised this checklist for my clients in new relationships, but some of these qualities are also important in the long term.

Key signs of trust in a person

They're open about themselves.

They're not evasive; they don't keep big, dark secrets. They don't vanish into the bathroom for hours with their phone. If you ask them a question about their past, they'll look you in the eye and give an honest answer. They talk about themselves freely and easily – but they don't hog all the airtime either.

They're interested in you in a balanced way.
They show genuine interest in you: who you are, what you do, where you've come from, and what you're into. They ask good questions. But they're not all over you, interrogating you, searching out your secrets and vulnerabilities, and squirrelling them away to use later (against you).

They have a life (so it's not going to be all about you).
They have friends/people and activities they enjoy, and want to spend time with and do. They don't immediately shape their whole life around yours. It's good to be loved unconditionally, but it's draining to have to provide a life-support system for someone else.

They respect your boundaries and priorities.
A healthy partner will respect your boundaries; they won't walk all over them. For example, if you need space to yourself in your week, or if you need to take your time in the relationship, they'll be okay with it. If you have children outside of the relationship, they'll respect your need to prioritise them and their needs.

They're independent (in the way YOU value).
This is about YOUR values and where you're at in your own life. For example, if you want to be with someone who is financially independent/has a job/owns their own house, you're allowed to hang out for that. But beware of someone who's so independent that they keep you waiting for a text while they see their friends, ride their mountain bike, visit their mother and do a million other things, before getting back to you at midnight to see if they can come over.

They're not weird about sex.
They're open about their sexual preferences and needs – or as open as you can be early on. I remember one young man telling

me about the things he wanted his girlfriend to do in bed – but she was reluctant and he felt disappointed. I listened, trying not to show my surprise. We all have our own views on 'normal', so let's just say there were clear reasons she would say 'no' to his suggestions. Just know that, if it feels weird or wrong to you, you don't have to do it. Or you can stop doing it. And your partner should respect your choice.

They manage their emotions – especially anger.

Managing all negative emotions healthily is a high bar to set. We all have moments we'd rather forget. It's hard to know how people manage themselves early in a relationship but, for a sneak peek, watch how they manage their work stress, frustration, disappointment and anger. Do their moods swing wildly? Do they have healthy ways of calming themselves down? Out-of-control anger can be dangerous but, even if it's not physically harmful, it's emotionally taxing and scary to be around. In the early days, if there's no sign of anger, ask them how they manage when they feel stressed, then wait to see if their behaviour matches their words. And also watch what they do when you have a disagreement. A person's go-to conflict style is revealing. (More on that in the Conflict Skills chapter, see page 95.)

Other people trust them.

This is a huge clue. You have the impression that other people (such as their best mate, friends, co-workers, mother) wouldn't hesitate to trust them with a big secret, knowing that they'll keep it safe.

This is a reliable reverse indicator, too. If you get the impression other people don't like or trust them, take note.

They align with the things that matter to you.

You don't have to be perfectly matchy-matchy on all your values – such as religion, culture, sex, marriage, kids, money, which country/town you want to live in, use of drugs/alcohol/porn – but being generally compatible helps. For example, if you want kids and your partner absolutely doesn't, don't expect them to warm up to the idea. Same with marriage. Or changing religion. I've had several clients park these issues early in the relationship, only to have them come back and bite them (to the point of breakup) later on. Have the big conversations as early as it feels appropriate.

They're thoughtful, in a consistent, behind-the-scenes way.

Thoughtfulness comes in all sorts of packages. From being nice to your mother, to giving you a foot massage after a tough day, to anticipating what might make your life a little sweeter BEFORE you've dropped 1,000 hints. A lack of thoughtfulness will erode goodwill in a relationship. But a person who makes an effort for you, without expecting fanfare or payback, is gold. Especially if – as the weeks, months and years pass – they keep it up.

What does a healthy, trusting relationship look like to me?

There are many variations on what 'healthy and trusting' means. I once had a client who worked up a spreadsheet so he could rank the qualities of all the people he dated, ruling them out if they didn't stack up. I don't advocate for that method – it's too prescriptive. And a bit mean. Love isn't a tidy package; if you look too hard for one, you're bound for disappointment. Not to mention missing out on some people who would make excellent partners for you.

Trust comes down to the deals you strike together – these don't have to be the same as your parents, your best mate or the person next door. The key is in the clarity of the lines you draw. One woman, whose partner wanted an open relationship, felt confused. 'I'm open to it,' she said, 'but how do we know we're together? How do I know I'm a priority? How do I know I'm not just giving her a leave pass to screw around?'

Good point. Agreements need to be made about money and vices, substances and alcohol, use of porn, work and leisure time, and chores – and especially sex. The estimates on infidelity, for example, vary wildly. Some studies claim that about 14 per cent of people in established relationships cheat; others indicate that the figure is as high as 70 per cent. But in whether it counts as 'breaking trust' is a matter for the couple involved.

We all need a place to start. I've helped many clients to develop their own lists, including their dealbreakers – the things they absolutely can't live with. For example, if your mother's alcoholism left you scarred, being with a heavy drinker is going to traumatise you. Even being with a moderate drinker may stir up difficult feelings. Be warned.

Let's examine the key signs of a healthy, trusting relationship. These are the gold standard, but human error means that even the most devoted partner will break trust from time to time – they'll forget to send text messages, turn up late, forget to pick up milk on the way home … so a little latitude is allowed.

This list is written from the point of view of one partner (you), but you can quietly use it to check out your partner's qualities, too.

Key signs of a healthy, trusting relationship

My choices line up with the agreements we've made.
This assumes you've made some agreements, particularly about your vulnerable areas. Beyond that, it refers to the choices you make when you're NOT together. You don't give them cause to doubt you.

Our approach to sex is aligned.
Due to its potential to cause conflict, sex needs a category of its own. It's important to have your own set of sexual 'rules'.

Questions can include: *How do we define being faithful (consider flirting and electronic messaging, especially text messages and sexting)? How do we define cheating? How do you feel about 'open' relationships/threesomes? How do you feel about keeping secrets? What's your attitude to same-sex friendship? Porn?*

Remember: Even open relationships need boundaries.

I feel safe to be vulnerable.

Sex is always consensual – every part of it. You respect your partner's needs and desires. You don't feel afraid of each other. You aren't constantly worrying about what mood the other person is in. You can both be fully vulnerable physically, sexually and emotionally. You can blurt out all your inner crazy, without being crushed or laughed at (at least not in a mean way).

I give my partner space to express themselves.

There's an open, easy flow of information between you. You ask questions, and you listen respectfully. You don't interrupt with fascinating titbits of your own. You don't cut each other down or belittle their views. You both feel 'heard', even if you don't always agree with each other.

I don't want to break into their phone.

Technology, particularly phones, has bred a culture of mistrust in relationships – with good reason. It's easy to hide messages, but it's also easy to be caught. Trustworthy partners are chilled and open about their relationships and friendships. You don't have to fret about who's texting your partner and they don't have to worry about you.

I like what I've got.

You accept and appreciate your partner and all their foibles. (Note: This shouldn't mean you've just given up.) Some things you can't change in a partner, such as their history, their regrets, their families, the people and 'stuff' they are drawn to, and their addictions/compulsions. You can buy them a new pair of jeans or nicer undies, or suggest a different hairstyle, or even help them find another job but, beyond that, you need to tread lightly. I always remind people to be careful about dating someone's potential. You need to like the raw material, knowing, in essence, that's who you're going to be with.

I take responsibility for my 'stuff'.

You don't expect your partner to monitor your drinking, drugging, spending or porn watching, or how much you work or your moods. And they don't expect it of you. You are equal partners, not leaning posts. You run your life well, and you own your mistakes. When you mess up or upset your partner, you acknowledge it – and, where appropriate, you make a sincere apology.

I build my partner up, especially in vulnerable areas.

You lift your partner up; you definitely don't drag them down. A young woman struggling with her body image was terrified about being naked in front of a new partner. She told him about her anxiety, she made excuses to not be intimate, she turned out the lights, and she got undressed in the bathroom. Flippantly, he told her not to worry about it and left it at that. He gave no praise, no reassurance, nothing to make her feel okay. Wrong move, and uncaring. This opened a divide between them that they couldn't recover from.

I express love in ways THEY like.

You know how your partner likes to receive love (e.g. a cuddle, cuppa, adventure, gift, hand-written note, time together) and you strive to meet their needs, rather than stick to what YOU like to do best.

We can sit in easy silence.

This doesn't mean post-conflict silence, or emotional shut-down silence, or we-have-run-out-of-things-to-say-to-each-other silence. This is comfortable, easy, I-know-you're-there-but-I-don't-need-to-talk silence. In other words, you feel at peace with your partner; it's not like an emotional bomb is about to go off or you need to apologise for something. Comfy silence is trust at its best.

I'm loyal with our 'dirty laundry'.

Here, I don't mean keeping deep, dark secrets hidden or never talking about your relationship to your friends. However, your first loyalty is to your partner; you don't rip them to shreds in front of others – and you refrain from doing it behind their back, too.

We can count on each other.

For time, support, empathy, compassion and friendship. You always have each other's back.

I'm free to be myself.

Your partner's not possessive of your time and energy. They don't try to control your friendships, what you like to do or who you hang out with. When you open up and say what's in your heart, they listen. They support you. They cheer you on. They don't criticise or make fun of you. They want, and encourage, you to be yourself. Because you're the person they want to be with.

#2 Trusting yourself: Who are you really?

Now, let's turn to the trust you have in yourself. Self-trust is the foundation of any relationship, including (and most importantly) the relationship you have with yourself. After all, you're the only person who'll never leave you.

Having self-trust means that you function well in a relationship, that you feel secure and independent, knowing your relationship adds to your life, rather than desperately needing it. A solid foundation of self-trust is also extremely helpful for when things go wrong, such as going through a difficult period in your relationship, or a breakup. Even if it's tough, your trust in yourself will help you recover. So it's vital to nurture your self-trust and, if you're a little low on it, to commit to building it.

Here's a quiz to check in on your level of self-trust, followed by a case study and the principles of self-trust.

**

How to know you trust yourself

Answer 'yes' or 'no'.
- *I'm not afraid to be open with my partner.*
- *I don't assume everyone I meet has bad intentions*
- *I'm able to fully relax when I'm in a relationship.*
- *I make decisions without seeking multiple reassurances.*
- *I'm generally good at reading people. I usually get it right in friendships.*
- *When I've made poor choices with people, I make an effort to understand why.*
- *I'm present in my relationship, not focusing too much on its future.*
- *I generally choose good friends.*
- *I'm able to trust a partner when they've given me no reason not to.*
- *I maintain my own friends and independent interests when I'm with someone.*
- *I'm relaxed about my partner maintaining their own interests/friends.*

- *I'm not excessively clingy.*
- *I'm able to express my needs honestly to my partner.*
- *I'm able to appreciate my good qualities.*
- *I'm able to take (genuine and fair) criticism from my partner.*
- *I accept compliments graciously and without question.*
- *I'm compassionate with myself.*
- *I back myself to leave a relationship that is bad/unhealthy for me.*
- *I like who I am.*

Results

If you found yourself saying 'yes' way more than 'no', you're in good shape. Either you haven't been too badly hurt, or you've been able to come back from it. Or, if your circumstances have been difficult, you have coped well. You have a good baseline for self-trust. You know what to do – you just have to keep doing it.

If you struggled with your answers, it's okay. It's also understandable if you've been hurt by someone you trusted, especially if it's happened more than once. The important thing to know is that trust issues can be worked on and overcome. The following story illustrates this with some tips to help.

Insecurity in relationships: Chase's story

Chase, 29, is worried about his relationship. In the six months he's been with his girlfriend, his personality has changed. He's quieter, more anxious. 'I'm usually pretty confident, but now I'm a clingy ball of anxiety,' he says. 'I'm not the guy she started dating. But I don't want her to know that, so I'm putting on an act. It's stressing me out.'

He's had a few casual girlfriends but, this time, Chase has fallen hard. 'I can't stand the thought of losing her, so I can't relax and enjoy being together. My head gets into a spin, and I start thinking I don't deserve to have her. Or that she'll leave me. I'm hopeless at this.'

Chase has fallen into a classic insecurity trap. The more you become attached to someone, the more you have to lose, and so the more you try to make it secure by controlling it. Your partner begins to feel smothered and backs away, causing you to cling tighter; the relationship loses its lightness and cracks appear.

Chase explains that his father had cheated on his mother with several women, and his parents had been through a traumatic divorce. He's worried about heading the same way.

But when we broke it down, the picture looked quite different. There was a logical four-step story to his difficulties:

1. His parents' divorce had made him feel anxious about relationships generally.
2. He was inexperienced in relationships. He'd finally met someone great, but he didn't know what a healthy relationship looked like or how to play it.
3. He was not at all like his father, in looks, personality or how he saw the world. He had never cheated.
4. He wasn't hopeless – he was anxious. His insecurity about losing his girlfriend made him jealous (when there was no reason to be) and he picked unnecessary fights. He thought it would be easier to lose her because he'd behaved badly than to be rejected for who he was as a man.

To his credit, Chase was able to see how his insecurity had set up his unhealthy behaviour. He could then see himself with more compassion and begin to reframe his view of his relationship. A year on, he felt secure and happier with his girlfriend.

***

Relationship insecurity is common. It needs to be worked on because it has the power to derail even solid relationships.

While it often shows up in new relationships, as in Chase's case, it can also persist or flare up after you've been together a while. It may be due to a loss of confidence – perhaps you've been out of work and/or home with kids, gained weight, been unwell or just lost your mojo. Perhaps your partner's life has taken an upswing – they're out socialising and meeting new people – and you're feeling left behind.

When this happens, it's important to take an honest look at what's going on, so your worries don't take over. Here are some tips for building yourself up.

Building self-trust: The key principles

Don't believe everything you think.

Sometimes, our minds are mini-monsters. They can take us into places we have no right or need to go. Don't buy into the truth of everything that passes through your head – some thoughts are dumb, wrong and mischievous. It can be damaging to cling to them. Especially, don't react on the strength of these thoughts. Step back, pause and look at the evidence. Chances are, you will react quite differently if you give yourself time.

Be vulnerable by small degrees (or take your time getting to know someone).

If you barely know someone, you don't have to drop your emotional guard altogether. Let it down slowly. People take time to reveal themselves. Wait to find out the truth of who you're with. There is no absolute timeline, but love has a funny way of sitting in our blind spots. Take notice of any big red flags. Sometimes, our own insecurity can cause us to over-invest in (or cling to) someone who isn't the right person for us. Take your time.

Learn your body's physiological signals.

If you let it, your body will often tell you what's going on for you in the context of your relationship. Learn to read the signs – especially anxiety. Being with someone shouldn't make you feel edgy or scared. If the relationship is right, you will slowly start to relax.

Make life decisions without seeking multiple input.

Sometimes, we need another person's opinions, but often we don't. Wherever you can, practise making decisions by yourself. This doesn't mean constantly over-ruling what other people/your partner wants to do, but being clear about your own needs rather than always going with the flow. Say 'yes' for yourself – and 'no' too.

When you make a promise to yourself, keep it.

If you said you'd go for a walk this evening, why are you lying on the couch? If you said you'd go to the movies with your friend tonight, why are you cancelling to be with your partner? Trust begins with yourself. If you make a promise to yourself, get behind it.

Put eggs in other baskets.

Don't count on your relationship meeting all your needs. Your relationship is not your life's work – it's a partnership. Invest in your own interests/friends. This is your insurance if things don't work out. But more importantly than that, these things are who you are. Hold on to them.

Be bolder in your life outside your relationship and bank your progress.

Take mini-risks, wherever you can. Try new things. Meet new people. Then congratulate yourself for your boldness.

Take compliments shamelessly (not gloatingly).

This one doesn't need an explanation. And if your partner never compliments you? Hmmm.

Advise yourself like a best friend.

People who feel insecure in relationships are often wise counsellors for their friends. That's because they have thought (and read) so much about relationships, so they understand what's going on and know what to do. Question and counsel yourself as you would your best mate. *'So, Jemma, tell me more about this.'* Then stop beating up on yourself for being anxious and go do whatever it is you've told yourself to do.

Use your strengths and gifts.

Hopefully, you know what these are. We all have a unique collection. Use them, daily if possible. Because that's why you have them. And using them will remind you of the person you are.

My personal strengths are:
1. ....
2. ....
3. ....

Write down all you have to offer as a partner.

When we're feeling insecure, we often lose sight of this. Write down your best qualities, everything you bring to a relationship, and keep it in your phone to refresh your view of yourself, or give yourself a boost. It's okay to ask your partner too – most will be happy to share their thoughts.

My best qualities as a partner are:
1. ....
2. ....
3. ....

Embrace the risk.

A long time ago, a friend asked me if he should ask his girlfriend to marry him. In my early 20s, I knew nothing about relationships, so I said blindly: 'Why not? Life's a punt. You can't get the good without risking the bad.'

He married her and, it turns out, my advice wasn't that great. But I wasn't wrong about the risk. Everything in life is part punt. Loving someone doesn't come with a warranty. Remember, however, the risk you take should be a calculated one. Not everyone is amazing. Not everyone is good for you. But someone – somewhere – will be.

Surviving a relationship crisis: Maia's story

A relationship crisis – such as an affair or betrayal – often brings people to therapy. If you've found yourself there, just know that you can, and will, recover. Let's hear from Maia.

***

Maia can't decide if she's sad – or absolutely furious. A few weeks earlier, her husband Jonny had told her he was no longer in love with her. Since then, she's swung between bouts of sobbing and wanting to kill him. Not literally, of course, but you know what I mean.

Emotionally, Maia is struggling to hold it together. As she slumps down on my couch, I ask her what Jonny not being 'in love' means for them. Stony silence? Couples counselling? A genuine effort to put things back together? She shakes her head. 'He doesn't want to try. He just wants to move out. I don't know what he expects marriage to be, after 12 years together and two kids. Some bloody fairy tale?'

Maia says Jonny's declaration seemed to come out of the blue.

He'd showed no clear signs of unhappiness. He was grumpy – but he has a stressful job and works long hours, so it wasn't unusual. 'It just seems so unfair. He never said anything was wrong, so I didn't even have a chance to work on it. Surely, he could have talked to me?'

She says, as far as she knows, there's no other woman. I try to prepare her gently for the idea that there could be – a new person, or the promise of one, is often the catalyst for a breakup. She hopes he will change his mind. He doesn't. The following week, they tell their kids, and it breaks everyone's hearts. He moves out. They share caring for the kids. She begins to shuffle forward. Two months later, her six-year-old tells her about the 'nice lady' Dad has introduced her and her brother to.

Maia is furious all over again. She's hurt he could give up on them, and the future they'd planned, so easily. She's also worried about money – Jonny earned a lot more than she did – and how her kids will handle a divorce.

She swipes bitterly at the box of tissues on the coffee table. 'I'm not worried about having the kids on my own. I did everything anyway. But I feel like a failure. I'm nearly 40. All I wanted was a good marriage and happy family. I never wanted to be a divorcée. I never wanted this for my kids. What am I going to do?'

Here are the survival keys for people like Maia, who are going through a breakup following betrayal. While they clearly relate to infidelity, you can swap in any experience in which someone has betrayed you.

When it's over: A survival guide

Is it over?

In Maia's case, it was definitely finished. Infidelity doesn't have to signal *The End*, however; depending on the circumstances, the relationship may still be worth saving and working on. But if you decide to stay together, get some help with mapping out a recovery process, because ongoing paranoia, resentment and anger are difficult for everyone to live with.

Hit the reality button.

Denial is a part of the process. Some days, you'll wake up wondering if the betrayal was all just a dream (okay, nightmare). It wasn't. It happened. The first step is to acknowledge the reality of your new situation. Get the professional (including legal and financial) help you need. Writing yourself a plan can help you see things as they really are. From there, you can make sound decisions about what you need to do now, and later.

Anxiety is part of the deal.

When people talk about the flood of emotions that accompany betrayal, they'll roll with shock, sadness, confusion, anger, shame, resentment and even depression. Those feelings are all valid. But when you work with people struggling with betrayal, you learn that anxiety is the biggest player of all. Even if you weren't an anxious person, betrayal turns you into one. You may find yourself worrying (or panicking) about everything: What to tell the kids, your choices, your state of mind, seeing your ex with their new love, what it all means for your future. It's tough, but you need to know that anxiety, in all its disguises, is normal.

You don't have to hold their secrets – but be careful with your story.

If you've been cheated on, it's tempting to tell the world. After all, why should YOU take the rap for THEM? Why should you pretend it's mutual or that the relationship just broke down? That's a fair point; you are under no obligation to 'hold' secrets for someone who's hurt you. But before you go public, consider the bigger picture. If you have kids, you may be hurting them. This might not be the right time to 'tell all' – consider waiting.

Work out what breakup story you want to tell for now and stick to it.

Choose your language.

Swear all you like, but be careful of pegging yourself as a victim because it will keep you stuck. So don't keep saying 'I was dumped' or 'They left/cheated on me.' As soon as you can, just say 'We broke up' or 'It's over.' From that point, you can begin to tell yourself it was for the best (and it was for the best if that person doesn't want to be with you).

Know who to trust and unhook from the rest.

Whenever you go through any Big Life Stuff, it changes your relationships. You learn who's in your corner, who wants to be but can't face it – and who's not. That's okay, people are just people; sometimes, they have their own valid reasons for not supporting you. The only people you need to detach from are those you don't trust: those who could hurt you, gossip about you, or make you more distressed/anxious than you already are. For your own sanity, walk away from them or block them. And lean on the people who are there for you – they're gold.

Don't be mean to yourself.

Being betrayed is like having a fire lit beneath your self-doubt. People often beat themselves up because they didn't see the cracks in their relationship, or the signs of cheating. They also worry about what they did wrong or what's wrong with them. Even if your relationship wasn't great, you don't have to take the blame for a choice your partner made. Be gentle with yourself. And, if that feels out of reach at the moment, lower the bar. Just don't be mean.

Detach from bitterness, because it'll take over.

I recall a woman who I saw 12 years after her husband cheated on her. He'd had several partners since he'd left her and the latest one was pregnant. He was NEVER coming back. But my client stayed in the gap between hope (that he'd return to her) and bitterness (because she knew he wouldn't). She still lived the half-life she'd developed after he'd gone. It was beyond sad: 12 years is a long time to shape your life around someone who barely thinks about you. Whatever you do, walk away from bitterness. It can dictate your life.

Choose freedom (over the other crap).

It's devastating to be hurt by someone you loved and trusted. If you decide to forgive, however, you (both) have to throw your whole hearts at it. Spending the rest of your life checking your partner's phone isn't freedom. Worrying if you're 'good enough' for them isn't freedom. Numbing yourself with drugs, alcohol or food isn't freedom. Hating them for hurting you isn't freedom. Freedom is believing you could have a good life without them.

***

There's a postscript to Maia's story. Three years after she and her husband separated, she returned to see me, because she was 'ready but not desperate' to start dating again. She and her kids were doing well. It had taken time, she said, and been gut-wrenchingly hard at times, but she'd been able to see her marriage as it really was – far from perfect. Her ex-husband's partner was pregnant, she told me with a grin. 'It hurt at first but now I almost pity her. Let's hope he does a little better second time around.'

Trust: Quick takeaways

- How you trust is the bright yellow signpost to how you love.
- Trust isn't always broken in *Shock, horror!* ways, it can be eaten away by 1,000 tiny cuts.
- Acknowledging your history is healthier than running from it.
- People only show us what they want us to see; they reveal themselves slowly. Take your time.
- If you've been hurt, be compassionate with yourself.
- Walk away from bitterness, because it has the power to shape your life.
- Love's a punt: you can't get the good without risking all the rest.
- Having trust in your partner is great.
- Having trust in yourself is gold.

PILLAR 2:
COMMUNICATION

How do you connect?

'The greatest compliment that was ever paid me was when
one asked me what I thought, and attended to my answer.'
– Henry David Thoreau

Why does it matter? Communication allows you to express
your needs, beliefs, thoughts and feelings to each other. Healthy
communication promotes connection, trust and intimacy. You
won't go the distance without it – not happily, anyway.

***

Poor communication is a trouble-maker in relationships. Many
studies cite it as the number one reason couples split, followed
closely by the inability to resolve conflict. For many couples, these
amount to the same thing.

When you're having ongoing communication difficulties, it can
be tempting to blame your partner or fling the relationship into
the Too Hard basket. Maybe that's where it ultimately belongs,

but first, you need to take an important step, which is to analyse how you interact – how you express yourself – and why. If you understand this, you'll get on better with your partner, as well as kids and other people in your world.

In this chapter, we'll delve into your interactions and explore some of the stickiest issues for couples, before considering strategies to boost your communication skills. To kick things off, the following case study illustrates one of the most common communication breakdowns.

'We've lost our connection': Ryan's story

Ryan and his partner Ali have lost their connection. They've been together for 15 years; they have two kids, two dogs and a hefty mortgage. From the outside, they're a strong, middle-class family unit, probably the envy of many of their friends.

In the past year, however, Ryan says he's felt a gap open up between them. The usual niggles about housework and parenting, as well as having no time to themselves, have turned into big arguments, followed by sulks and uneasy truces.

'I love Ali. She's a sexy woman and a great mum to our kids. When we're good, we're really good. But lately, we're sort of missing each other. We're there, but we're not. We're not connecting.'

'Have either of you been under more stress lately?' I ask, by way of reminding him he'd booked the session to discuss work stress.

'Yes, but I can't dump all the blame on work. When I try to talk to Ali about us, she won't give me a straight answer. Then she goes quiet and gets on her phone. After a while, I just give up. Speaking of that, she's ALWAYS on her phone. I can't compete.'

'Is there anyone else in the picture?' I ask. The obvious question, given the mistrust people have about their partner's constant phone use.

He shakes his head. 'I don't think so. Unless she's fitting them in between Pinterest and Instagram. I just think she's lost interest – in sex and me. She doesn't talk to me beyond the stuff with the kids. She doesn't even seem up for trying. I don't know if we're going to make it.'

But we used to talk all night …

Like many couples who've been together a while, Ryan and Ali are feeling their relationship drift. There's been no dramatic event or massive row. It's just that time and life (and technology) have led them into the 'We don't talk anymore' zone. Interestingly, it's always about talking. No-one ever says 'We don't listen anymore' or 'We've stopped listening to each other.' Which might be more helpful.

'We were once so good together,' Ryan says sadly. 'It's hard to believe we're the same couple.'

But it's not hard to believe when you consider the reality of a long-term relationship. Stress, life struggles, distraction and fatigue all take a heavy toll. The cliché – that we take our stress out on those closest to us – is a cliché for a reason: It's true. Just as we share all our good news with our partners, we take home all the crap, too. At our worst, we find a way to blame them for it.

Ryan was nostalgic for the beginning of his relationship, which started out pretty much the same as everyone else's. Bright-eyed, staring into each other's eyes, feeling a beat of excitement every time a text message pings, talking about *Everything*.

It's not possible, of course, to sustain this. We get busy, we get tired, we get bored and, after 15 years, we don't feel thrilled and grateful to be with this person. We certainly don't want to stay up all night talking to them. Why would we? We know their history and all their 'stuff', and we can't stand the thought of going through it all again BEFORE having to have sex –

especially after midnight, when the kids might wake up. Like Ryan, you start thinking you've lost the urge to talk, but it's not that, it's just that the content isn't fresh anymore. It's not sexy or exciting; it's domestic and dull. You tell yourself you're no longer on the same path but, in truth, it's the opposite. You're on SAME DAMN PATH and the idea of staying on it wants to make you scream.

So, if you've found yourself here, where Ryan and Ali are, take a breath. You can rejuvenate relationships that have grown tired, and you can find and strengthen connections that have been lost, if you are willing to try.

Communication 101: It's not easy

In relationships, communication transfers information – thoughts, feelings and views – between the parties. Which is a lot. No wonder it's hard.

But there's no hiding from it, either. Unless you live alone in a remote cave and never come out, it's impossible *not* to communicate. We communicate in the way we talk (and listen), our choice of words and how we deliver them, how we move and walk, our facial expressions and gestures, our behaviours, our digital communications – impulsive, random and habitual. We communicate via the things we don't do and say, too.

All this is just one side of communication: Our side. The other side is how it lands. Even if we've conveyed our message well – with the perfect wording, a big smile, and in the right spirit – we can't be sure how our partners will receive it. We can't know how they'll decode the message, or how they'll react to it. And that can cause problems. Especially in a world where electronic messages are so easily misinterpreted.

How do you communicate?

Dr Gary Chapman popularised the idea of communicating through love languages (*The Five Love Languages*, 1992). He identified these languages as physical touch, words of affirmation, acts of service, receiving gifts and quality time.

This classification remains useful in helping people understand that we give and receive love in different ways. While a hug may be your favourite thing, your partner may prefer a funny card or spontaneous coffee date. Based on all I've seen and heard, however, there's no replacement for time – time spent together will show up the quality of the relationship, for better or worse. That's why so many people have struggled with their relationships during the pandemic lockdowns: They brought them face-to-face with reality. *Is this who I really want to be with? Or not?*

Time gives you space to talk and work through problems. Equally, people who have no time together – or when they do, it feels rushed or squeezed – will almost invariably feel a disconnect, which cools the atmosphere between them.

But back to talking, our primary means of communicating. We need to dissect *how we talk* to our partners: the tone, volume, warmth (or ice), choice of words – those we use and those we leave out. Whether we talk a lot, say nothing or want to say something – but can't. I ask my clients how they talk to their partner, but I don't always need to because it can become obvious during the session. I recall one man who leapt in to finish ALL my sentences for me. (Silent note to self: how annoying would that be to live with?) Or the woman who threw icy water on every one of my suggestions to stop her from feeling resentful about doing housework. Even if they were bad suggestions, which I accept was possible, how would this go down with a partner?

Some people think they're slick communicators because they flew through a Communication Styles test at work. This makes me smile – how you need to interact at work isn't necessarily how you should at home. For a start, your partner isn't your direct report, personal assistant or even client, and you're playing with an inferno if you treat them that way. Plenty of highly successful leaders have, let's say, 'unenviable' relationships. And plenty of their shy, quiet employees have warm, loving domestic relationships. Go figure.

The first problem is that most takes on 'communication styles' have been designed for the workplace. The second is that the term 'styles' is too rigid. It assumes you don't have a choice in how you communicate, when you mostly do. I prefer 'bias' because it suggests you lean towards a particular way of interacting, but you can be flexible when necessary, which is key to relationships.

These are the six most identifiable biases in relationships.

The six communication biases

All classifications have their limits, but these are a general guide. Most of us adopt different biases in different situations, or depending on our mood at the time, but you should be able to identify the one you most often lean into, and maybe a back-up one, too.

Understanding your communication bias gives you insight into how you're sending messages and how they might make your partner feel when they land. It can help you identify your triggers as well as those of your partner. Most of all, it can help you choose how you want to be in the relationship and how you want to treat your partner.

Here's a description of each bias, along with their key positive and negative attributes.

Assertive

Dominant

Open-expressive

Passive-avoidant

Passive-aggressive

Open-erratic

Assertive

Descriptor: *This is the way I see it, what's yours?*

Assertive communicators express their views clearly, directly and with respect – which is an asset in relationships. People with this bias tend to be emotionally consistent and can manage their ups and downs well. They don't get swamped by emotion when trying to get their feelings across. They speak up for themselves when they need to, but are also open to criticism and are capable of listening to their partner's views and struggles. In an ideal world, we'd all be assertive communicators all the time, but it's not an ideal world and few of us are perfect communicators – not consistently, anyway.

Positive: Can balance intellect with emotions when expressing themselves. Listen well and can accurately gauge where their partner, or relationship, is at.

Negative: None, apart from being hard to pick a fight with them.

Dominant

Descriptor: *My way or the highway.*

Dominant communication is aggressive, usually driven by a person's need to be right, be listened to, or get their own way. This causes problems in relationships because dominant communicators tend to be poor listeners and struggle to see things from their partner's perspective. Dominance is closely linked with control which, for obvious reasons, isn't healthy in relationships.

Note: A bias to dominance is more extreme than 'bossiness', which often develops from the need to 'get sh*t done' and keep life running smoothly, which – let's face it – every household needs.

Positive: Will leave a partner in no doubt of what they want. Can be helpful in ensuring decisions get made, things get done and domestic life stays on track.

Negative: Bossiness at best. Controlling at worst. And poor listeners.

Open-expressive

Descriptor: *Let's tell each other everything.*

Open-expressive communicators tend to be warm, heart-on-the-sleeve type people, who lay everything on the table: their thoughts, feelings and everything in between. They have an intuitive radar for what's going on for others, which makes them caring partners. Open-expressive communicators have high levels of emotional reasoning, which means they tend to believe their emotional reactions prove something is true – even in the face of solid contrary evidence. Because they're led by their emotions, they're warm and loving when feeling good but, when they're not, they can overreact or spiral into negativity, which can be hard on relationships. In striving for openness, they may over-share, unintentionally saying hurtful things.

Positive: Believe in honesty and openness, and share what's going on for them freely. Up for supporting their partners 100 per cent.

Negative: Because they are so expressive, they expect their partner to be the same and can become frustrated with someone who struggles to do this. Regulating or controlling their emotions can be difficult for them.

Passive-avoidant

Descriptor: *Everything's just FINE.*

Avoidant (or passive) communicators struggle to express/articulate their views, or lack the confidence to ask for what they want, so they end up saying little or that everything's fine – even when it's not. Avoidance may come from insecurity, shyness, or it may just be that they are not skilled at expressing their feelings. While an avoidant approach might keep a lid on conflict, avoidant communicators can become resentful because they don't 'have a voice' in the relationship. And their partners may become frustrated in being with someone who won't say how they feel.

People who are in difficult, or toxic, relationships can become passive-avoidant over time, which can make it difficult for them to stand up for themselves, even when it's required. When people move from avoidant to submissive, they are probably being bullied, if not physically then emotionally.

Positive: Non-confrontational. Tend to be easy going, accommodating and go-with-the-flow types. Often the family peacekeeper or mediator. Won't nit-pick.

Negative: Conflict avoidant, so may let things slide when they need to be addressed. Their own needs may get put aside, especially if they're with more assertive partners, which can lead to resentment.

Passive-aggressive

Descriptor: *Let me show you how I feel.*

Passive-aggressive communicators deploy resistance as their primary tactic. Instead of being openly angry, upset or frustrated, they'll show their negative feelings through their behaviour. For example, they may procrastinate, shut down, be stubborn, be sullen or sulk. The goal is to let their partner know they're unhappy and, often, to make them suffer because of it. So they may deliberately delay a job they know their partner wants done. Or they'll just go quiet and leave their partner to figure out what's up.

Passive-aggressiveness may develop over time when people are unhappy but can't express themselves healthily.

Positive: Superficially calm, as in no yelling matches.

Negative: It's hard to know what's upset or really going on for them. Conflict is not addressed, it just shows up in their behaviours, mood or general unhappiness, so relationships can stagnate or deteriorate.

Open-erratic

Descriptor: *I can't tell you what's coming because I don't know either.*

Open-erratic communication is high-level unpredictability. With an open-erratic communicator you'll never be sure what you're going to get or, if it's you, your partner won't be sure who's coming home to them. This bias indicates an unstable history, and people who have this often unconsciously create turmoil, because it's what they know best and where they feel comfortable.

Open-erratic communication can be manipulative but, because it can also switch to loving, it can be hard to figure out, which leaves partners confused and anxious. Their partners often say they're 'walking on eggshells' and living in a state of low-level anxiety.
Positive: Affectionate, can be socially charming and popular.
Negative: Unpredictable. Impossible to read. Emotional roller-coaster for partners.

***

Analysing your bias
Most of us are up for claiming our more positive attributes and passing quickly over the negative. But it's still worth thinking about how you communicate with your partner, and whether it's helping or hindering the relationship. Which most applies to you?

1. *My primary bias is* ....
2. *My secondary bias is* ....

Most of us are a cross-blend; we're not consistent either. Just as an assertive communicator can occasionally lash out, an avoidant person can promote harmony, and an erratic communicator can be loving. Sometimes, how we communicate is about the dynamic between us and our partners – whether we clash or complement each other.

Being in a difficult relationship can change how you communicate, while a stable partner can help to calm and bring out the best in you. For an example of a clash, see the case study (Nat's story) that ends this chapter.

***

Sticky issues: Top communication problems for couples

Couples vary, but communication problems tend to show up like a playlist on repeat. These are the problems psychologists most often hear, and they stack up with the research, too. So ignore them at your peril!

Communication problems include:

- not truly listening (being distracted)
- not being able to articulate feelings
- misinterpretation (e.g. making assumptions and jumping to conclusions)
- fixating on an issue
- defensiveness/blaming (e.g. using 'you' statements, instead of 'I' or 'we')
- letting emotion take over
- interrupting/overtalking
- avoidance (of anything hard or big).

Maybe you recognise some of these issues in how you interact with your current partner or one you have had in the past? If so, read on for some tips about resolving or at least managing them.

1. Not (truly) listening, or listening on the run

In a world full of distraction, where there are so many things vying for our attention, this has become a huge issue. Raise your hand if you focus 100 per cent on your partner – you'll definitely be the only person in the room. Or country. Attention economics suggests human attention is a resource, and we only have so much of it. That's true, but only giving people – especially partners and kids – scraps of your attention sends the message that what they have to say is not important or interesting to you.

TIP 1: Write yourself a list of the five people who truly matter in your world. This sounds obvious, but a list ranked in order of importance (don't worry, no-one else needs to see it) helps to clarify things in your own mind. When you're with those people one-to-one, sit down and slow down. Look at them and focus. Top marks if you're listening well enough to give relevant responses to what they're saying.

TIP 2: Agree on rules about phone use (and pledge to stick to them). Studies show more than half of people in relationships complain their partners spend too much time on their phones, and one-third of all couples use electronic devices in bed. It's hard to be persuaded that this is a bonding experience.

2. Difficulty expressing/articulating feelings or needs

It's important to say what you want and need in a relationship. Often, difficulties arise when people expect their partner to have read their mind. But some people find this incredibly stressful and shut down in the face of any conflict. I had one client who literally couldn't speak when his wife criticised him. This infuriated him because, at work, he was confident and articulate. But an unhealthy pattern had set up between him and his wife, which meant they couldn't discuss any irritants without silence or a blow-up.

TIP: If you have difficulty with verbal expression, or you get upset, write things down before you discuss them with your partner. It will help clarify what you want to say. There's no shame in taking a list to a relationship 'meeting' if it helps you both communicate better.

3. Misinterpretation

This covers the whole gamut of jumping to conclusions and making assumptions. It has always been a source of trouble between couples, but technology has further complicated it.

Misunderstood text messages and emails cause a lot of arguments. Couples in long-distance relationships, particularly, will vouch for this.

The No. 1 rule for therapists is don't make assumptions, because you don't know for sure what's going on in the person's heart and mind. The same should apply to relationships.

TIP: Talk with your partner about relationship boundaries and expectations early – or refresh them often. Give your partner the benefit of the doubt, unless a dysfunctional pattern has set in. Don't rely on text messages to communicate, especially not to settle an argument. Text fights leave everyone feeling upset. So talk. On the phone. Or in person if you can.

4. Fixating on an issue

This is common when one partner has betrayed the other, and the hurt partner finds it difficult to let go. The slightest provocation or reminder – or even a stressful day – can trigger an argument. It can also occur in the most basic annoyances (such as how someone loads the dishwasher or your partner visiting his mother five times a week). Repeat arguments – where the same issues flare up – are exhausting, and they will gradually erode whatever goodwill you have together. Be careful with this one.

*TIP: If you find yourself obsessing on an issue, you need a **process and strategies** to work through these issues. If your own research doesn't help, it's worth asking a professional.*

5. Being excessively defensive/blaming

The problem here is taking criticism, even mild comments, as a personal attack. It can take the form of blaming or accusing a partner, to shift the focus away from themselves. In defensive mode, you'll tend to say 'you' instead of 'I' or 'we'. Defensiveness is often the result of being heavily criticised in childhood or as a young person. When a person is repeatedly defensive, their partner may shut down and adopt passive-aggressive behaviours as a way of being 'heard'.

TIP 1: Tap into your physiology. Allow yourself to feel the physical response in your body before you speak. Is it really anger? Often, it's not anger, it's fear. Fear that you won't be loved, or you'll be left, or you're not good enough. Recognising fear or anxiety helps you to be compassionate with yourself, and reminds you that you're no longer that hurt child or adolescent. And that your response can be different.

TIP 2: Assume your partner's comments/actions are coming from a place of love. Or their own fear. This will (or should) take the heat out of your response.

6. Letting emotion take over

This is about being more emotional than the situation reasonably requires. Your feelings overwhelm you and govern your actions, instead of being able to balance emotion with rational thought. This may be because you (or your partner) struggle to regulate your emotions. Or you have a highly emotional go-to response to stress or arguments.

TIP: When you're upset or annoyed, it's important to hit the pause button (take some time out) so you can think about your response, instead of acting on impulse and lashing out. Sit (or even lie) down and breathe until you feel calmer. It will help you respond more rationally.

7. Interrupting/overtalking

You can't just talk your relationship out of trouble. If only. Talking at length may not help you feel connected – it may even make things worse, because the same old problems are raised but never fully settled. They're just put on the back burner until someone strikes another match.

It can be hard to know if you're talking too much –

sometimes, it's just to compensate for being with a quiet partner. Or needing to be heard and valued. But if your partner raises this as a problem between you, listen, because it can make a huge positive difference.

TIP: Easy. Okay, not so easy if you're a talker. But silence truly is golden, so shut up for a bit and listen. Practise silence. Let your partner fill the airtime. Sometimes, I sit in silence for agonisingly long periods with my clients. Any discomfort is almost always mine. Eventually, they talk. And I'm always amazed by what they say, and what I learn.

8. Avoiding the 'hard' or 'big' stuff

Sometimes, either you or your partner struggles to say what you want/need in a relationship (or what you don't want). Either the topic is avoided or if the topic is raised, it causes an argument. Chronic avoidance often leads to a sad breakup or a relationship filled with resentment.

TIP: The only thing you need to know is that avoidance doesn't make difficult issues go away. It just leaves them to simmer in the background, so no-one gets any peace. No matter how hard it is, you need to speak up for what's important to you. Otherwise, you're just putting your life on hold. You'll find more on this in Finding Your Voice (see page 87).

The negativity effect: A subtle warning

Do you walk on the gloomy side of life? Negativity deserves its own category as a communication problem. It can drag promising relationships into the dust bowl because it's so draining to live with.

The Negativity Effect is simply a bias to negative or pessimistic thinking, over positive or neutral thinking about (1) yourself, (2) other people, and (3) the world generally. This has a flow-on effect on relationships.

I've had a number of clients who struggle with negativity (or their partners have) and are at a loss to know what to do about it. I admire someone who steps up to address their negativity, because it's usually an ingrained pattern of behaviour that takes effort to shift. But I've seen some great turnarounds by people who are genuinely up for doing things differently.

How to know if you're too negative

We all have negative thoughts, but chronic or habitual negativity can affect your everyday function, quality of life and mental health. It's important to distinguish chronic negativity from healthy expressions of sad or negative emotions, and genuine mental struggles such as depression and anxiety.

Obviously, negativity can escalate during tough times or when someone is mentally unwell. A chronically negative person will consistently demonstrate six or more of the following signs:

- Take small slights or suggestions from a partner extremely personally.
- Always expect the worst to happen day-to-day and possibly in the relationship.
- Filter out positive events/interactions to focus on negative ones.
- Frequently pick arguments over small issues.
- Be moody or grumpy with partner and family.
- Be hypercritical of others – with partners often at the top of the list.
- Greet partner's ideas with a reason they won't work, or say 'no' to suggestions before even considering 'yes'.
- Overthink everything (e.g. ruminating, excessively picking over conversations or interactions).
- Struggle to give genuine compliments or praise.

- Tend to believe others don't like you, even when there's no supporting evidence.
- Struggle to find enjoyment in everyday things.
- Blame others, including partners, for many things.
- Find it difficult to recover from disappointment, rejection or bad news.
- Find it hard to see yourself in a positive light.

How to turn negativity around

Chronic negativity often has long, gnarly roots, which can be tracked to your childhood or emotional history. You can't help that, but it's worth striving to turn it around because there will be a marked difference in your life and relationships.

Even if you're not especially negative, you'll find some tips in here that might apply to your own situation.

1. Take a PAUSE.

Negativity is often driven by anxiety – rumination about what went wrong in the past or concern about what could go wrong in the future. When we feel anxious, we often think we must either (1) express it, or (2) do something with it. This leads us to respond or act too quickly. So WAIT before you speak. Give yourself time to assess whether you really need to raise that grievance. Is it THAT important? We can let go a lot of minor issues if we take time to think, to be reasonable.

Pausing is a great strategy all round; if we give ourselves space to cool down and think, it's remarkable what we can let go. Everyone should have a Pause button in their communication toolkit.

2. Examine your thoughts for truth/validity.

Let's say you've just told your partner the new picture they want to hang on the wall in your lounge will look bad. Examine your thoughts. *Is it true? Do you know that for sure? Even if it does look bad, doesn't your partner have the right to find this out for themselves? And if they love it and you don't, why can't it hang on the wall, anyway? Must the Sole Rights of Home Décor rest with you?*

Remember, your strong opinions are not necessarily grounded in truth. Even when they are, they are YOUR truth, which may be quite different from that of your partner. So practise seeing theirs.

3. Don't aim to be positive.

That's like telling someone who'd die for chocolate cake to give it up altogether. It's too hard and just ramps up the craving. Instead, aim to be open-minded. When your partner makes a suggestion you don't like, force yourself to stay open to possibility. Tell yourself you're an 'open-minded person' and tell others, too. It's an attractive quality (as long as you mean it).

4. Give a compliment or praise.

This is a MUCH better strategy than trying to be positive. It may feel foreign at first, but persist. If it's genuine, you'll create goodwill for both you and your partner.

5. Check your complaining.

About your work, your boss, your health, your frustrations, the weather, the chores, the toaster settings, who moved your cheese …

We all need to vent at times, so your partner will hopefully be up for listening to your genuine worries. But, beyond that, no-one needs to hear all the negative contents of your mind. Not even you. It's fair enough to have such thoughts but, well, get a journal or a dog. If you're good to your dog, they'll love you unconditionally. But don't count on the same from anyone else.

6. Negativity doesn't make you seem clever.

Negative people often believe their responses will make them look clever because they've seen what no-one else has – how everything could go wrong. In fact, the opposite occurs. A person who habitually responds negatively is often seen as intellectually rigid, or even limited, rather than clever. As having one fixed view – your own. This will give you less power in any relationship. Wouldn't you rather be seen as flexible and open-minded?

7. What would your life look like without it?

Imagine a life free of negativity? Okay, that's unrealistic. We all get low and gloomy sometimes; the great wash of life can be tiring and testing.

But a life free of **habitual negativity**? More friends, more success at work, more (positive) attention, better relationships, more opportunities, more fun. Isn't that an incentive worth chasing?

Emotional intelligence helps communication – and everything

'… emotional intelligence is not the opposite of intelligence,
it is not the triumph of heart over head – it is the unique
intersection of both.'

– David Caruso

Happy couples aren't smarter, wealthier or more resilient. They don't necessarily spend more time together, share more interests or have a better regime for dividing chores. They don't sit around endlessly staring into each other's eyes; they may bicker as much as any other couple. But they have one thing that keeps them from sinking into the mire of battle or discontent – emotional intelligence (EQ). As relationship expert Dr John Gottman notes,

EQ is the 'surprisingly simple secret' to making an intimate relationship work. It's the key predictor of whether a couple will stay together – happily.

***

EQ is a person's ability to notice, manage and express their emotions healthily. This has implications for trust, intimacy, conflict management and, obviously, communication. In short, it makes the whole deal easier and more fun.

Conversely, relationships that lack EQ will struggle. Niggles or disagreements blow out into massive fights, distance will creep in and anxiety will bubble constantly beneath the surface.

High EQ communicators have a sound grasp of the *emotions and intent* in interactions. In relationships, they know the importance of making the other person feel understood and valued through words, body language and behaviour. The reason they're so good is that they practise these things, often to the point of automation.

Based on research and clinical observation, this is what high EQ communicators do.

1. Display positive regard: I like you.

This is just a research-based way of saying you each like the other – and you show it. If you like someone, you want (and try harder) to engage with them in positive ways. And if you believe the other person likes you, you're far more inclined to speak and behave warmly towards them.

The same is true in reverse, too. When there's a feeling of negativity – especially when it stretches out over time – it will disrupt even the best efforts at positive interaction. Further, liking your partner hugely boosts your willingness to engage with them, and willing engagement is essential in resolving conflict or even just being together comfortably.

2. Tune into their partner's efforts to connect: I'm here for you.

Gottman describes a person's efforts for attention, affection or acceptance as 'bids for connection'. These might be a question, touch, text message or casual comment about anything from the weather to the weak plotline of a movie made for TV.

It's almost impossible to respond to every one of these bids, but emotionally skilled partners have a high success rate. They'll lean in more than they lean out, they'll say 'yes' more than they say 'no'. This doesn't mean they're downtrodden, nor do they compromise their own wellbeing to put the other person first, but they make a genuine effort to connect and, where possible, to make their life a little sweeter.

3. See their own imperfections: I know I've screwed up.

Lots of people believe they are self-aware but – unfortunately – it doesn't always stretch as far as knowing what they're like to be with as a partner. Being a 'good person' doesn't necessarily mean it's easy to be in a relationship with you. Being able to see your flaws and mistakes accurately, understand what triggered or led to them, AND being up for making a genuine apology (without prompting or bribing) is crucial to good communication. It's also easier said than done.

4. Show vulnerability: I'm struggling and I need your support.

Are you open and honest with your partner about what's going on for you emotionally? This doesn't mean being excessively needy, voicing every worry that comes into your head and seeking constant pick-me-ups. It means having a healthy, communicative response to your struggles – letting your partner know what's going on BEFORE you shut down or erupt.

To show vulnerability is to be honest about distressful thoughts, feelings and circumstances, and voice them in a way the other person can understand. Relationships often suffer from one partner 'not having a clue' about what's going on for the other. You shouldn't have to mind-read to get to the core of your partner's struggles and they shouldn't have to figure out yours.

5. View the world through another's eyes: I get you.
Listening skills always (and rightfully) get a big rap. But good communication is about more than listening. It's being able to show you have (1) heard what your partner is saying, and (2) genuinely understand things from their point of view.

There's another sneaky pathway to this: the ability to hear what's NOT being said. To intuitively understand your partner is struggling and gently draw them out, particularly when emotional expression doesn't come naturally or easily to them.

Being able to understand each other is not just a sign of a healthy relationship, it's the key to heading off – and resolving – niggly issues and conflict before they embed themselves between you.

6. Regulate their emotions: This is what the situation requires.
EQ is about being able to acknowledge and express tough emotions without being gridlocked by them; it's about being able to pick yourself up, calm yourself down and move forward when the time is right.

When you combine heart and mind in your communications, your feelings don't dictate your words and actions. You don't speak impulsively in ways that seriously undermine the relationship. You make accurate assessments of situations, which make it easier to come up with a healthy response.

More communication tips from the trenches
Here are some generic tips for improving communication, raising awareness of your partner's needs, ensuring your own voice is heard in the relationship.

1. Set a regular 'chat' time (so it's not driven by emotions).

When we raise issues with our partners, it's often out of frustration or, worse, we've reached emotional boiling point. So, our words come out with anger and tears. But if you can say what you need, quietly, clearly and reasonably, you are FAR more likely to be listened to.

A young man I worked with uses a WMC (Wednesday Marriage Chat) to talk things through with his partner. He says it's 'been amazing' because it offers a regular, neutral space for each of them to say what's up, rather than storing things until they're at lashing-out point. They make sure they talk about the good things, too.

Many experts cite the importance of couples having a regular check-in time – and a weekly chat is less onerous than date night. To get the most out of it, however, you should agree on some rules.

Wednesday (or any night) marriage chat: suggested rules

- Catch up once a week, trying to keep the time regular. Same time, same place if possible – and prioritise it.
- Keep it short – 20 minutes is enough and agree that, when time is up, you'll move on to a different topic.
- Don't have the chat over a drink if drinking is a conflict trigger for either of you. Alcohol frequently is.
- Take five minutes each to speak. Don't speak when the other person is speaking (unless to affirm you've heard them!). Then use the other 10 minutes to discuss. Use a timer if you need one.
- Validate the other person's problems. (Use their words, not yours: *Yeah, I can see why you're having such a shitty time.*)
- Don't offer unwanted advice.

- Discuss the good things about your week as well as the struggles.
- Always end on a positive note.
- Don't overrun the amount of time you've agreed on and don't pick up where you left off later that night. Keep it contained. If an issue is still bubbling, you can return to it next time. Or you can save any grievances until then.

2. Don't share Every. Single. Thing.

I know this flies in the face of 'honesty' in a relationship, but trusting each other doesn't mean full disclosure of every thought and feeling. It also doesn't mean being 'selective' about the truth or telling little white lies whenever it suits you. It means that the entire contents of anyone's heart and mind are jumbled and boring – so edit yourself. Share the things that matter most.

3. Don't use your partner as a vessel to vent.

Not too much, anyway! Most of us like (and need) a vent, particularly when we're stressed. And those we love are often the best – and most tolerant – of this need. Your partner should support you, but take care to make sure they're not just a dumping ground for your stress. Partners can suffer from secondary stress when you keep piling the same issues on them, such as your work stress, or your difficulties with a manager, or your mother. Make sure you have other, healthy ways to let off steam.

4. Be specific about how they could help you.

This doesn't mean 'be bossy'. But it's smart to avoid saying vague things to your partner like *'I need you to do more,' 'I'm unhappy with this situation,'* or *'I want you to initiate things.'* These requests may sound reasonable, but they lead people to feel helpless or hopeless because they're not sure what to do to make things better.

If you want more help, ask for it in specific terms. *I'd like to carve out some time for myself on Fridays. Could you please drop off the kids on Wednesdays and Thursdays? Could you take over the cooking on Monday nights?* You may not get an immediate 'yes', but it's a better starting point for domestic negotiations.

5. Listening is more important than talking.

This is the golden rule for success in any relationship, including parenting and friendships. You already know what you think; let others have the airtime so you can learn what's going on for them.

Finding your voice

'50 per cent of a great relationship is how you treat someone.
The other 50 per cent is having the ability and confidence to communicate the treatment you want in return.'

– Matthew Hussey

Having a voice in your relationship is absolutely critical, because that's how you express your needs to your partner.

Many people shut down their voice (thus putting their own needs on ice) because they don't want to cause drama and conflict. It's a poor strategy, however, because it doesn't clear the air, it just compresses it, until something rips the tab off and a fight blows up.

Lots of people lose their voice when they're with a dominant partner. It's understandable: It's anxiety-provoking, or even frightening, to be vulnerable with your needs when you know you'll be overruled, ridiculed or laughed at. When people have come out of toxic relationships, they often need help to find – or rediscover – their voice.

Here are some examples of situations I've encountered, in which couples have found their partner avoiding, shutting down or postponing the conversation. All couples in these examples were in committed relationships; all said they loved each other, but they couldn't discuss these issues. It led to either avoidance or a fight.

- *You want to open a joint bank account.*
- *You want to travel before settling down together.*
- *You want to talk about getting married/starting a family, or having kids at all.*
- *You need to make a decision about which country to move to/live in.*
- *You want to talk honestly about a problem in your relationship.*
- *Your kids have left home: you'd like to travel but your partner is a homebody.*

When is it time to worry?

Some struggle with anything that signals the relationship is entering the serious zone, or with change. Even the thought of it makes them uncomfortable.

These things may be understandable and, to be fair, one partner may not be in the same place in the relationship as the other.

The red flag is not that one partner doesn't want the same things as the other – it's that they've shut the gate before the other has even had a chance to explain their perspective. I recall one situation in which the man, in his late 50s, wanted to travel. He'd had a health scare and was worried time was running out. But his wife refused to talk about it. On the surface, it appeared she was being selfish but, when we unpacked it, she'd been so worried she would lose him that she couldn't bear to even think about doing anything differently. She needed to keep everything the same to manage her anxiety.

In another situation, a young woman told me her partner of several years wouldn't marry her – he had valid reasons for this relating to his own traumatic family history.

She said he was a great guy and supportive; they had a really good relationship. She didn't want to get married straight away, but it hurt her that he refused to discuss something that was important to her. It was the only real conflict they had.

'Am I *being unreasonable*?' she asked.

I couldn't answer that. It's impossible (and unfair) to make a call on someone else's relationship, primarily because you don't have to live with the consequences. But what I could tell her was that the most important thing in a relationship is to have a voice – to feel safe and able to speak up about what matters to you. Because, if you don't, you risk building your relationship on a foundation of resentment.

If you and your partner disagree on the Big Stuff, take this test before you decide to walk, or stay.

How to test your partner on the things that matter

1. Say clearly what you want.

Often, people hold back on what matters to them. This can be for a raft of reasons – most of them rooted in the fear of what their partner thinks, or what it might mean for their relationship. So speak up, calmly and clearly. If you struggle with this, write down a few bullet points to guide what you want to say. Give your partner a chance to hear what is important to you. Allow yourself to hear yourself say it out loud, too.

2. Find out what's fuelling their views.

If they don't want the same thing/s, ask them WHY they think the way they do. Do they have a history or past experience that has led them to think this way? Have they been traumatised in this area? If so, you need to absorb where they are coming from and the reason they think differently from you. At the very least, it tells you what you need to know to make an informed decision.

3. Check your view is reasonable.
Check what you are asking for is reasonable. If you're not sure, get some neutral advice. For example, if you want a family and your partner has never wanted kids, then you might be being unfair in expecting them to change their mind midway through the relationship. (This issue is increasingly common, by the way.)

Or if you're wanting to open a joint bank account, and you have a bad credit history or a load of debts from a gambling habit – well, you can understand their reluctance, can't you? At least, I hope you can. Be fair. And be aware that if you badger someone for something they never wanted, it's unlikely to lead you down a happy path.

4. Explore a compromise/set a deadline.
Is it possible to meet somewhere in the middle? Can you find an outcome (or set a deadline) you'd both be happy with? If so, great. But be wary of just putting things 'on hold' because it's likely that over more time, and with more stress, you will both become more attached to your own view. If you absolutely must put things on hold, set a time to have another discussion. Then it won't keep coming up on a daily basis – you can relax until the deadline rolls around.

Remember, the most important thing is NOT to get your own way. It's to make sure you can clearly express what you want. That your partner respects you enough to listen and understand your views. And that you respect them enough to do the same.

A clash in communication bias: Nat's story

Nat has signed on for therapy because she's hit a wall with her partner, Aaron.

At 37, she's a successful professional; she spends most weekends hiking or biking, and her social life hums. 'Meeting guys is easy,' she said. 'But I can't seem to keep it going. Is it them, or is it me?'

Nat and Aaron have been dating for six months. Mainly, it was fantastic, but something is bothering her – and she's been there before with previous partners.

She describes a recurring pattern with communication. 'Aaron's fun but he's the strong, silent type emotionally and it drives me crazy. I can't ever seem to get guys to open up to me. And I need that – I'm a talker. I need it all on the table.'

'And Aaron isn't up for that?' I prompt.

She shakes her head. 'He talks but he keeps it light – a lot of banter – and I can't get a handle on how he's feeling about anything. I just want him to say what's going on. But when I try, he clams up. It's like talking to a rock.'

I wait, because I know she's about to drop the $50 million question.

'How can I get him to open up to me?' she says.

It's a common struggle, in which one partner is open, while the other is closed. Research shows it's healthy to talk about feelings – that even being able to name a feeling can reduce its intensity and help us to better manage it. But when one partner is (way) more up for talking than the other, it can cause anxiety and tension. It's frustrating to be with a 'silent' partner when you like to talk.

Nat needed a lot of reassurance about the relationship. It made sense given that, for all her popularity, she'd never been able to make a relationship work. And she'd come from a family which validated her athletic ability and grades – but not her personality or feelings.

Her need for Aaron to speak up was less about what he was feeling, than what he was feeling about her and their future. When she didn't receive reassurance from him, it caused her anxiety to escalate which, in turn, made her even more fixated on getting a response from him. This made him withdraw further and caused friction between them.

'That's exactly what's happening,' Nat says. 'So how can I do things differently? How can I ease the tension?'

Here's how. While these tips are for Nat and others like her, they can be applied more broadly to your own situation, to gauge how you and your partner express your feelings.

How to check in on your emotional expression

1. Rate your own emotional expression (EE).

Rate your ability (and that of your partner) to express your emotions (i.e. your EE score). Use a scale of 1–5 (where 1 = Finds it difficult to express emotion, and 5 = Very open in talking about feelings). Notice the difference between the two of you, knowing that it's fine – possibly even healthy – to be different.

2. Ask WHY you want to know (how they feel).

BEFORE asking what your partner feels, be honest with yourself: WHY do you want to know? Often, asking your partner how they feel is less about them and more about relieving your own insecurities through talking to someone. That's not fair. Your partner should support you, but not be constantly badgered to reveal their feelings just to bring your own anxiety down. So check in on your reasons and make sure they aren't fully motivated by your own insecurity or worries. Are you thinking about your partner's needs, too?

3. Ask WHY your partner may be quiet.

The reality, however, is some people find it extremely difficult – even painful – to express their emotions. It's just possible that your stream of questions, or those of a former partner, or even a parent, have hammered them into silence. Or their early environments meant they never learned emotional skills or language. They may need time, and your understanding, around that.

4. It's okay to not know everything.

You don't need to know EVERYTHING that's going on in your partner's head. If you did, you might be shocked. Or bored. Or feel something unpleasant. A little silence is okay. It can be peaceful and energising for your relationship, too.

5. Read the room.

Talking is not the only way to identify your partner's feelings. In fact, it's not the most reliable method. If you want the good oil, check out their behaviour. A person's body language – how they react and what they choose to do – is hugely revealing. Pay particular attention if you notice a CHANGE in a person's behaviour, because that may indicate a change in their emotional state.

6. Clock their behaviour towards YOU.

Rather than trying to access your partner's feelings, consider how you are treated in the relationship. Are they loving and kind? Considerate? Do they bring good energy to the relationship? Do they want to spend time with you? Do they support you, go out with you, introduce you with pride, and are by your side for the events that matter? Those may be bigger clues than what they say.

***

People communicate the way they do for all sorts of reasons. You don't have to try to dig out the roots of it. You don't have to justify their quietness – or their drama. Nor do you have to resign yourself to it. If telling them how you feel doesn't change things, ultimately, you need to ask yourself: Does this person, with their way of functioning, work for me? If your answer is 'yes', go all in. And if it's 'no', you know what you need to do.

Communication: Quick takeaways

- It's not just about the message you send, but how your partner **feels** when they receive it.
- What you DON'T say or do is a powerful message, too.
- Your partner isn't your direct report or personal assistant. Beware of their reaction if you treat them as though they are.
- Giving a compliment is a better strategy than trying to be positive.
- Work on your emotional skills (EQ) – they're the surprisingly simple secret to happy relationships.
- Being able to hit Pause is almost as important as listening well.
- Your dog will love you unconditionally; but don't count on it from anyone else.
- You don't need to know the entire contents of your partner's mind – and they don't need to know yours.
- Showing your partner you like them is the underrated key to successful relationships.

PILLAR 3:
CONFLICT SKILLS

Do you fight healthily?

'If you don't have conflict, you don't have intimacy.'
– Clinical psychologist and
Holocaust survivor Dr Edith Eger

Why does it matter? Conflict is human nature, and a part of nearly all intimate relationships. Being able to deal healthily with a disagreement creates understanding between you and can bring you closer. There's a toxic side to conflict, however, which we'll explore in more detail in Part 2: Toxic Conflict (see page 127).

***

PART 1: HEALTHY CONFLICT

According to family folklore, my grandparents 'never had a cross word.'

That's what everyone said, and that's how it looked – and felt – whenever we visited their house. They were just two people living in harmony: he trekked off to the coal mine each morning; she had a hot dinner ready for him on his return. He happily weeded the garden; she hummed as she peeled the potatoes. If they were ever outraged or upset, if they ever fought, no-one witnessed it.

It was only once I became a psychologist that I questioned this image. Were they for real? Did my grandmother never erupt over the endless domestic chores? Did she never lash out about giving up teaching to run a house and raise a family? Did my grandad never feel resentful that he worked so hard and never struck paydirt? Or get stressed about money? Or yell at the kids? Did they really live so peacefully, or were they really simmering with discontent? Were they the ultimate emotional bottlers?

If it was luck, they had a massive dose of it. If I heard a couple say that now – *We've never had a cross word* – I'd be asking: Who are you? Have you even been living in the same house? I mean, who hasn't got into a 'heated debate' with their partner, called them names, cried, sworn, sulked, stormed out, slammed the door – or all of the above? Who hasn't had outbursts they regret, or have shoved in the Things I'd Rather Forget file? The point is this: couples fight. Being a good partner is not about never fighting or getting angry. Anger is a normal human emotion and suppressing it can fuel anxiety and other mental health struggles. Yes, some ways of airing your grievances are better than others. But conflict is part of the intimacy package. When it's handled well, it can clear the air, enable you to see each other's perspectives, and build trust and closeness – all of which lead to growth.

In this chapter, we'll take a look at what couples commonly fight about, how much is too much, and we'll identify your go-to conflict style using the Conflict Wheel. Finally, we'll consider the conflict traps to avoid and provide strategies for moving off the battleground into a healthier place.

But let's begin with Jason, who had found himself gridlocked in conflict and was blaming himself for the mess.

***

Going into battle: Jason's story

Jason wants to know if the conflict in his relationship is normal.

He's extra worried because he's in his third marriage – and he knows the divorce statistics rise with each subsequent union.

Jason's first marriage ended because they were too young. The second ended in a 'shit storm' over money and custody of the kids. Now, the third is heading down the same track. The gaps between fights are getting shorter, the silences longer. There is little fun and about as much sex.

'There's no getting away from it,' he says, miserably. 'The common denominator in these breakups – this conflict – is me. I need to do something.'

Jason says he's never been physically violent, but his frustration is pushing him to the edge. He's had to leave the house and run down the road to calm himself down.

He describes a relationship that can go from relaxed and jokey to screaming and yelling in a flash. He's constantly on edge, waiting for the next outburst. He feels his partner pushes and goads him until he snaps; he feels constantly criticised and blamed.

In spite of that, he adores her. She's the love of his life. He's desperate for it to work. 'Besides, I can't afford another failure – financially or mentally,' he says. 'Help me.'

***

Clearly, Jason's relationship is in trouble. He and his partner could probably benefit from couples counselling, but she refuses to attend. She says he needs to work on himself and his anger problems first, especially with children in the house.

That may well be true, but I always raise an eyebrow when one partner 'sends' the other to therapy. In doing so, they're loading the blame and responsibility onto one player, when there are two in the game.

I've had plenty of clients who've been sent to therapy with an ultimatum: 'Fix yourself or else.' One woman who'd been given this command described an emotionally abusive relationship – she gave so many small, clear examples of her partner's toxicity that they had to be true. He agreed to come to one of her sessions to fill in the blanks for me, because 'he knew her best.' When it came to his turn to speak, he shone; the words flowed. It was like he was born to the therapy stage. After the session, he sent me a long email. It was several carefully researched pages, complete with quotes, full of insights into their relationship. I assumed this was so I'd know who the more intelligent partner was.

I did know, and the more intelligent one eventually left him. It was not without a lot of tears and heartache for everyone, including their children.

While some relationships are not built to last, conflict is human. As Dr Edith Eger says, it may not be possible to achieve full intimacy without it.

Good partners fight fair – and healthily

Most of us know that we should fight fair but, in the heat of an argument, we're not jumping on the internet and researching how to do it. We should take time to learn, however, because while conflict can be healthy, it can also take a significant toll on our mental wellbeing. It can hurt the kids, too. We've all seen those movies where kids witness horrible marital fights from the staircase, then go on to be the heroes in their own story. But that's not how things really unfold. Most kids will survive a few parental scraps. But research shows that severe, chronic conflict between partners negatively impacts children. Just because you make a point of never fighting in front of them, doesn't mean they don't feel it. Kids sense tension and they can carry that fear forward.

When I hear clients describe bitter tensions between their parents, it reminds me that conflict has a legacy. One woman said her parents argued constantly throughout her childhood; they called it 'debating'. But it made everyone feel uncomfortable. 'I thought it was normal. I didn't know there was another way your parents could treat each other. It took me years to figure out – it wasn't debating, it was fighting. They're in their 70s now and they still do it. It still makes my stomach churn with anxiety.'

For all that, however, conflict is inevitable. Learning to work through it is not just helpful for your relationship – a healthy approach to conflict, and having the skills to manage it, are an invaluable gift to your kids.

The fight club: Charting your disputes

Identifying what couples fight about most is both easy and tough, depending on how you look at it. Statistically, any topic that can be discussed or debated can cause trouble. Which doesn't bear thinking about, because the list is too long.

Some topics can be reliably thrown on the table – especially if you're with someone for a long time. Here are the 10 biggest hot buttons, in no particular order. Use this list to map your pain points onto a graph like the one on page 102. It will help you to identify what needs most attention.

1. **Money** Always an issue. Being poor is stressful but having a lot of money can cause problems, too. Ask any wealthy couple who've been through a divorce. But it's often not so much the amount of money, it's the discrepancies in how we spend it (or want to spend it) that causes arguments. Clashes between spenders and savers are common.

2. **Sex.** Betrayal, obviously. But also sexual compatibility, which can change over time. Couples mostly fight about how often to have sex, which leads to resentment and/or guilt.

3. **Families.** Who wants to see who (and who doesn't), who's taking up more time than they should, who's causing trouble, who's coming to stay (for too long), and who we'll spend Christmas or holidays with. Couples who get on well with both/all sets of parents and extended families don't know how lucky they are.

4. **Chores.** The division of labour often, if not always, seems so unfair and causes resentment. It's not just doing chores either, but who's doing the household admin, who's calling the electrician, who's remembering which days the kids have a sausage sizzle, or who's picking up milk on the way home. Sigh. Cue fatigue. It's exhausting.

5. **Jealousy.** Possibly, one partner has given the other cause to be jealous. Or one person is feeling insecure in the relationship. This can play out in many ways, from a casual flirtation at a work party to messaging an ex on Facebook to sneaking to the bathroom with your phone. Be warned.

6. **Kids/parenting styles.** Differing parenting styles can be a huge cause of contention, especially when one side is authoritarian and the other leans towards permissive. Parents in blended families often struggle with this. But also just the presence of kids, and their needs, can lead to arguments. I know, we're not supposed to admit that out loud, because love and everything, but kids do cause us stress and worry, and it often lands heavily on our relationships.

7. **Time.** No-one has enough of the stuff. Getting no 'me' time is the source of many problems, especially when the other person seems to be having plenty of fun. Filed under 'time' is also how much one partner works when they could be at home. This can cause resentment, because it sends the message that work is more interesting and worthy than the person you're supposed to love. Oops.

8. **Technology.** Many people complain that their partner has a more intense relationship with their phone/laptop than they do with them. To be fair, technology has multiple uses – work, news, information, connection, organising 'stuff', shopping, entertainment and pleasure. So it's hard for an ordinary human to compete. But, if you're getting more fun from your phone than your partner, take note.

9. **Big stuff.** Religion, culture, where to live, politics, the future, whether to marry, commit, have kids, any addictions or health problems. It's a long list. It pays to have these conversations as early as possible in the relationship, or tend to them as they arise, because they're problems that bed in and don't go away easily.

10. **Past misdemeanours.** A quietly dangerous one. Anyone who raises the past in their arguments – especially repeatedly – is heading for trouble.

THE IMPACT OF CONFLICT

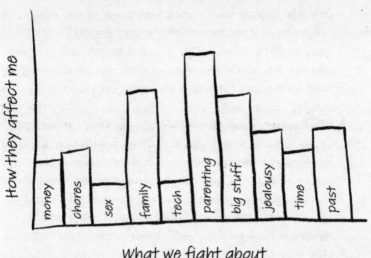

How they affect me

money · chores · sex · family · tech · parenting · big stuff · jealousy · time · past

what we fight about

Analysing your conflict

When you've completed your chart, take a moment to acknowledge your hot button(s). Again, it doesn't really matter what the issue is, as long as you can own it, talk about it and work out healthy ways of moving forward.

Perhaps the biggest clue as to the health of your relationship is *what happens between fights* – the tone and general vibe of your relationship. How you speak to and treat each other daily. Do you look forward to seeing each other? Do you have fun together, make joint plans? What is the atmosphere like in your home?

Being a good partner is about staying in the game, trying (most days) to make things better. No matter where you sit, you'll find strategies in this chapter to help.

When is enough, enough?

As in Jason's relationship, one of the biggest difficulties with conflict is knowing how much is too much: where, precisely, the battle lines should be drawn. It's not something we ask our friends. We might tell them our partner annoys us, or we've had a row, but we don't tend to reveal the specifics. We don't say: 'I hurled 45 expletives,' 'I called him/her a [insert derogatory word/s here],' 'I sulked in my car for hours with a king-size block of chocolate,' 'I didn't speak for four-and-a-half days,' or 'I refused to have sex for a month.'

The lines between what's 'acceptable' and what's not differ between couples and can also blur. I've worked with a number of men who've struggled with this, primarily because they are less likely than women to have gathered related intel, to have discussed the details of their relationships with family and friends. And, when you don't know, it can lead you to get it badly wrong or to suffer in silence. One man I worked with got all his relationship lessons from the TV show *How I Met Your Mother.* He quoted it liberally. His partner, with whom he was locked in battle was – understandably – sceptical about the quality of this advice. And eventually, he left him, so perhaps the show wasn't useful after all.

Another man suffered for 10 years in a relationship with his wife. He filed her screaming, wild mood swings, breaking household objects, binge drinking and relentless criticism of him under: 'We're going through a rocky patch, like most couples do.' This was sad, given his own mental health was crumbling.

Contempt between couples is the biggest sign of trouble (the No. 1 predictor of divorce, according to research by The Gottman Institute). Sarcasm, disrespect, condescension, hostile humour, sneering, eye-rolling and name-calling are all forms of contempt. The reason it's so poisonous is that contempt attacks a person's sense of self, which is difficult, if not impossible, to come back from. When a couple lands here, you know, even if they stay together, it's going to be a long and bitter ride.

As conflict lines blur, so do the dealbreakers. What's okay to one person may be horrifying to another. What's a mild tiff for one couple may signal 'the end' for another. The most important thing when you fight, however, is whether you FEEL SAFE – physically, sexually and emotionally. If you don't, tell someone who can help you.

When you're struggling in a relationship, it's common to say: 'We're not getting on,' or 'Things are a bit rocky.' But what does that really mean? Although every relationship is different, it's helpful to break down what you (each or both) need to work on, or what may need professional help. Sometimes, life stress and the circumstances in which we find ourselves are big players, and making a change in those areas can reduce the stress between you.

Is your relationship healthy? The front door test

A woman I worked with described her relationship as shaky.

She'd been with her partner for eight years. They were now considering spending time apart. Their disagreements over parenting – she was a stepmum to his daughters aged 15 and 12 – had escalated.

The constant bickering over the girls' behaviour had led to several blow-outs. Each person had said things they regretted – but they couldn't take them back. 'I'm not sure love's enough anymore,' she said.

I asked her how she felt each evening as she approached the front door of their home.

'Anxious,' she said quickly. 'I dread going inside. I never know what I'm going to get. Lately, it's never good.'

I've asked the 'front door' question to a lot of people, especially when their relationships are beginning to affect their mental health. It's a way of reading your mental state by paying attention to what's going on in your body.

This is not a diagnostic measure of relationship health; rather, it's a reliable indicator of your daily state of mind regarding your partner or whoever you live with. (Note: This is a general test – not one to run only after you've had a fight!)

The front door test

Let's say you've finished work for the day and are approaching home. (If you're at home during the day, you'll have to do this metaphorically.) Assume whoever you share the place with (your partner/kids/others) is inside. Ask yourself the following questions.

1. Scan your body.

Do you feel calm and pleased to be home? Happy to see your partner/the kids? Or only the kids? Do you feel tense and jumpy? Do you fear what will greet you?

Signs of anxiety or low mood will often show up physiologically as you enter a stressful environment. So, scan your body and take a read of what's going on. Better still, name the feeling: that will make it real.

2. Monitor how long the feeling lasts.

Just a few moments? All evening until you're in bed? Is how you feel entirely dependent on your partner's mood, or whatever dynamics have been going on before you arrived? Have you begun to shape your behaviour to deal with the domestic mood? Is this in a good way?

3. What's the vibe of your evenings?

Let's say there's just the two of you. Is the atmosphere light, enjoyable? Can you have fun together or sit in compatible silence (not just on your devices)? Do you LIKE being there (or are there others who energise you more)? Can you get through the whole evening without bickering?

4. What's one thing that would improve us?

Even if your relationship is okay, it's good to keep an eye on how to make it better. Quit checking emails after 7 pm? Turn off your phones at an agreed time? Agree on a movie to watch together? Not fall asleep with your mouth open after too many glasses of wine?

If things are a little rocky, is it possible to change that? For example, if your step-parenting is the main source of conflict, talk with your partner about what's going on and how it could be better. People often need professional help to navigate blended families, because it's challenging. I've seen couples 'in love' fall apart over battles with their kids.

Don't avoid difficult topics, because they gain momentum. Even if you don't want to hear their answer, it's information you need for whatever choice you make.

5. Take the weekend away test.

Time away together should be fun. But sometimes, couples have become so gridlocked in their issues that even a planned break (that once would have been fun) goes belly up. If you can't achieve goodwill or a sense of peace when you've put aside time for each other, take note. You're in the red-light zone.

The front door test results

How'd you go? Hopefully, your relationship got a pass mark.

People often think relationship happiness is founded on great, grand, money-fuelled gestures. It's not. True contentment is buried in the dust and dirt of daily domestic life. Keep an eye on how you feel, and how your partner feels, when you're hanging out at home. The truth lies behind the front door.

Analysing conflict: How do you fight?

So, how are you fighting? In the throes of conflict, it's not easy to analyse exactly what's going on. But if conflict is a problem for you, or is becoming one, it's worth reflecting on (1) how you fight, and (2) your own go-to style of conflict.

In the simplest terms, there are two kinds of conflict: (1) *Acute*, or arguments that blow up in the context of daily life; and (2) *Chronic*, or those that simmer and seethe, often for years. Both can cause problems in that when they flare, you both hold tight to your views, make no headway, and are left feeling frustrated and hurt.

While acute problems can often be settled relatively quickly, chronic problems may have deep roots and create logjams that are hard to get past. The challenging thing is that acute and chronic fights are often intertwined – heard of dragging up the past? So, these categories aren't specific enough to help you get to the core of what's going on. It's more helpful to break conflict down using these four elements, and answer the related questions as they relate to you.

- **Onset** What triggers the fight?
- **Frequency** How often does it happen?
- **Intensity** To what level does it escalate?
- **Duration** How long does it last?

1. Onset

This refers to WHY the fight starts. Is there is a clear reason or trigger for the conflict? Or has it blown in from nowhere? Is it less about you as a couple, and more about the fatigue or stress that one (or both) of you is under? Is there another party involved? (Fights about family are common.) Are the same issues triggering your fights? Is it a problem from the past (e.g. a betrayal), or is it a current issue (e.g. chores around the house)? Both of these can be worked on.

What causes me/us to fight?
....
Is it the same issue(s) on repeat? Is there a pattern to it?
....
Do I/we have a strategy to break the cycle?
....

2. Frequency

How often do you fight? Annually? Monthly? Weekly? Do you get long breaks between arguments, or are you more like Jason and his partner – the fights are like a rolling stone from which you get little reprieve? Also consider whether your conflict has changed over time. Or with stress or life circumstances, which may be valid reasons for an increase in your conflict.

How often do we fight?
....
Do I (mostly) start the fights? If so, why?
....
Does this feel like a healthy level of conflict?
(Do I feel okay about it or worn down?)
....
Would I feel happier if it was different?
....

3. Intensity

What form does your conflict take? Lots of shouting and yelling? Screaming? Tears? Shut down? Silence? Sulking? Storming out? Withdrawing or withholding sex? (Obviously, physical violence, or any situation where someone's safety is being compromised, calls for urgent intervention.)

How does our conflict look?

....

Is it an appropriate level of conflict for the situation?

....

Do I feel safe?

....

4. Duration

How long does it last? Is the fight settled successfully and put aside? Or does it simmer until enough time passes and you go back to normal? Lots of couples use the 'just ignore it' tactic, which means issues bubble on, inflaming again with the tiniest spark. Not all clashes need to be fully resolved every time, but you do need a healthy means of easing your tensions. Do you have good strategies as a couple?

How do we end or settle our fights?

....

How do I feel after our attempts at managing it? (This is the best clue as to whether you are dealing with it healthily.)

....

What else could I do/do differently?

....

The Conflict Wheel

Conflict is frequently talked about as something to be resolved; hence the term Conflict Resolution. This is an unhelpful approach in a practical sense, however, given that about 65 per cent of fights between couples are never fully resolved. The problem often rests more with how you express your disagreement and how you leave it.

A critical factor is your personal response to conflict. To explain this, I use the Conflict Wheel, which shows the most common ways people respond to conflict in relationships. To identify your style from one of the six on the wheel, consider your *first response* to conflict. Your mood, circumstances, mental health and various stressors can all alter your response, so let's assume your *usual* method. Check out the wheel and the descriptions that match each style.

The Conflict Wheel: Analysing your response

1. Protective

People with a protective response leap into defensive mode. Highly sensitive to criticism of any kind, they may lash out, compete or overreact to the situation. However, there's usually a reason for this response buried in their past and, once a protector understands this, they can learn to hit Pause, then change their response.

2. Emotional

Emotional responders, or 'feelers', are driven by what they're feeling, rather than a rational or logical approach. For example, they may respond with tears, shouting or extreme anxiety. While it's healthy to let out your emotions, it can be difficult for you to talk or articulate your views. Feelers need to work on balancing their emotions with what is fair and reasonable.

3. Internalising

Internalisers shut down during conflict. They struggle to express their feelings, usually because they lack emotional skill. Perhaps they may have never learned it, or they're extremely shy. A little internalising can be helpful because it prevents you from acting impulsively, but 'bottling' feelings is unhealthy because it can lead to using unhelpful coping strategies such as alcohol, substance abuse or eating issues. It can also morph into mental health problems, such as depression or anxiety, or an eventual explosion in anger.

4. Avoidant

Avoidants detest conflict; they'll do anything to get out of its way. This means that, not only do they avoid talking about problems, but they also won't find it easy to be part of discussions that can clear the air. They're hard to pin down – on anything. Even an apology can be hard to extract. The positive side is that it's hard to fight with avoidants. But it can create a conflict logjam that's hard to break.

5. Accommodating

Accommodating people tend to be pleasers; they like to be liked. They will often roll over or bend to their partner's view to keep the peace, or because they like to fix or 'sort' disagreements quickly. Not doing so makes them anxious. They apologise often, even when it's not their responsibility to do so. The challenge for accommodators is to disagree or express their frustration. They need to work on having a clear voice in the relationship – to be heard, rather than becoming submissive.

6. Collaborative

Collaborators are the easiest to be in a relationship (and fight) with. They're fair, flexible and compromise easily. Collaborators tend to be emotionally secure, so they see problems for what they are and don't take any criticisms personally. They also won't put up with unreasonable behaviour. Few people can maintain this position 100 per cent of the time – but it's something for us all to aspire to, or at least move towards.

***

You've probably identified with one of those responses. Circle yours here.

- Protective
- Emotional
- Internalising
- Avoidant
- Accommodating
- Collaborative

Although a collaborative response is aspirational, there's no absolute right or wrong response. There are right and wrong behaviours, however, and being a good partner involves steering clear of words/actions that hurt your partner or destroy goodwill between you. Those who avoid/internalise anger, particularly, need to work on healthy ways of expressing their feelings, because chronic emotional suppression affects both your mental health and that of the relationship.

But the important thing is to identify:

- how you respond
- how long you stay in that mode
- whether you are happy with it.

I want to reiterate the importance of looking at what's happening BETWEEN fights. Does the tension settle and return to a comfortable place? Do you (both) still feel happy to be together? Do you put energy into making the relationship work? If so, great. If not, consider how you could move in a different direction, or cut down the time it takes for you to let any problems go.

It's extremely useful to identify your predominant conflict style. This will help you to understand yourself in the heat of conflict and, therefore, be better equipped to de-escalate disputes or avoid travelling in a destructive direction you can't alter. It may also help you understand why your partner reacts the way they do.

Making things better

Conflict traps – and strategies to help

Even the best of partners has grievances, which we need to air from time to time. Sometimes at great volume. But if you want to avoid setting your relationship – and your future together – on fire, you need to play fair. Here are some traps to avoid and strategies to help.

Fighting dirty

Three of the most popular dirt-dragging strategies are (1) using a current issue to bring up a past mistake, (2) globalising your discontent (blowing a small issue into a massive one), and (3) attacking an aspect of your partner that's difficult for them to change (e.g. their personality). These strategies are always futile and often mean – not to mention destructive. Keep your fights out of the dirt zone.

*TIP: Think back to your last fight. Did you manage to keep it **current** and **specific**? What could you change for next time? Aim to use 'I' instead of 'you' statements, e.g. 'I feel frustrated when the dishes aren't done,' instead of 'You are hopeless around the house!'*

Using sex as a weapon

Using sex as a weapon is a manipulation tactic: sex is withheld or 'given' to get what you want. Or you have sex to distract your partner from an issue that needs to be addressed.

While it's most commonly seen as a female tactic, both men and women use sex as a weapon. I recall one man who'd make a decision every evening on whether to have sex with his wife based on whether she'd been 'good' that day. She became desperate to have the sex she didn't even want. Go figure. This tactic always backfires. It turns sex into something it shouldn't be – a punishment or reward. And that means it's always loaded.

TIP: Make sure sex is just sex. Not a bargaining tool. Be careful about ending your fights with sex. Conflict can ignite desire but, if it becomes a pattern, it may reinforce the conflict.

Having to be right

People who always have to be right tend to have fragile egos; they need to shift blame to cope with their insecurity. Accepting you are wrong, or at least that there could be another way of looking at the situation, is a strength – not a weakness.

TIP: Practise not always having the last word. It's fine to let your partner say their piece and leave it at that. They will feel heard, too.

Trying too hard to be nice

People who like to please have a hard time with this. Expressing irritation or frustration doesn't make you a bad person, it makes you a normal one. Being able to tell a partner how you feel honestly is a sign you care.

TIP: If you're not used to expressing anger, you may have difficulty working out how to do it and how much is appropriate. Or you may derail your attempts with tears. Write down your feelings first, try them on a trusted friend or, even better, a therapist.

Negative confirmation bias

When you're struggling in your relationship – niggling, fighting, bored, or just a bit over it – you start REALLY seeing the things that annoy you in your partner. And once you see them, they start to glow – softly at first, then they blow up like neon strobes in Times Square. If this is happening to you, remind yourself of all that's good about your partner. If that's hard, look for one thing. If that's hard, go back to when you first met them. If even that's hard – what on earth were you thinking back then?

TIP: Name your partner's top three qualities. Come up with recent evidence to support each one. Then practise bringing these to mind before you blow up or make a negative comment.

Blame-shifting

Shifting the blame onto your partner is sometimes justified, but never helpful. In toxic relationships, it's a manipulation tactic. Commonly, however, blame-shifting is a coping mechanism; the person shifting the blame is trying to preserve their own self-worth or ego, and isn't fully conscious that their logic is faulty.

TIP: Refrain from using the word YOU. It's accusatory. Own your poor behaviour. 'Sorry' is a powerful word.

Using your physicality as power

When one partner is much bigger than the other, conflict can feel terrifying to the more vulnerable one. Using your body is threatening, even if you didn't intend it to be.

TIP: When you feel a fight beginning to escalate, sit down. Encourage your partner to work on disputes when sitting down. I once had a client who sat on the floor when he felt himself losing control. It took away his power and his wife didn't feel so intimidated. He hated it, but it worked for them. Note: In couples therapy, I've seen many times over that it's hard to fight when you're holding hands.

Breaking your unwritten agreements

Plenty of couples draw up prenuptial agreements around money but very few sign off (officially) on the things that are dealbreakers for them, such as cheating, untreated addictions, using joint funds without discussion. We just assume. Or we wait till it happens. It doesn't matter what your agreements are, as long as you are both clear about, and okay with, what it means. For example, an open relationship is fine if you are both willing participants and you are absolutely clear about what that looks like for both parties.

TIP: Check in with yourself to refresh on what your expectations, boundaries and dealbreakers are, THEN discuss them with your partner.

Fighting 'under the influence'

This means under the influence of anything that won't take the conflict in a helpful direction – definitely alcohol and drugs, and potentially family members and friends. It's also not helpful to start a loaded discussion when you're highly stressed, fatigued or emotional.

TIP: If you have an issue you need to work through, book in a time with your partner to talk it out when you're relatively calm and free of other influences.

'Time-out' words

Sometimes, we find ourselves in the grip of an emotion that overwhelms or feels out of control, which can escalate a conflict in ways we later regret. We may do or say things we can't take back. Although we might not know how the conflict is going to play out, we can often feel the emotion coming. At that point, it can be useful to use a 'time-out' word to signal to your partner you're feeling this way, so they can give you space and possibly protect themselves. Some people call them 'safe' words, which is appropriate if there's a threat to anyone's safety. But people often just need time to cool off. A time-out word can act as an off-switch to prevent arguments from escalating. Any word is fine – one couple I worked with used 'Banana', another 'Code Red' – the challenge is remembering to use it when your emotions are taking flight.

Traffic light strategy

This is a useful strategy for figuring out if the disagreement can be settled or if you are bound to keep going around in circles. When an issue flares up, assign it a green or red light. A green light means it's a problem you can work through and make progress with; a red light means the fight is futile and you should step away, at least for now. For example, who scrubs the shower can be changed. Who drops the kids off at school can be changed. How much time you spend at work or on your devices can be changed. Your gambling habit can potentially be changed (with the right help). The affair you/your partner had five years ago is a red light: It can't be changed (only your mindset about it can).

People sometimes ask if there's a halfway house, as in an orange light. The answer is yes. These are issues that tend to arise over and over. They can be changed but may need to be parked until the time is right or you can get outside help. A clash over parenting styles, for example, can be improved but it may (and frequently does) need an external perspective.

How to spot cracks in your relationship – before they become canyons

All relationships have their wobbles; the challenge is to get to them before they become irreconcilable. Here are eight quick tests to see if your relationship needs attention. And if it does, there are tips to help.

1. The I've-got-news test

Something great – or just interesting – happens during the day or on the news. Your partner used to be the first person you'd rush to tell. But you no longer do that. Has someone else replaced your partner, even just in your thoughts?

TIP: Be honest about who you enjoy talking to most, who you go to with your best news/gossip. Is that something you need to change? Quickly?

2. The free-time test

You finally get a free weekend and your partner is free, too. You know you need some time together BUT you're not sure you want to spend the weekend with them. You'd rather be with someone else (heed an extra warning if it's a *specific someone else*) or see your friends or even be alone. If this is you, be careful – especially if you're aware your relationship needs attention.

TIP: Create a window of time just for your relationship (even a coffee date is a start), then do your best to be fully present during it … or be prepared for the distance to creep in.

3. The silence-is-not-golden test

You go out for dinner, and you're that awkward couple in the restaurant: You find yourself with little to say to each other beyond work, family and domestics. You take a short-term focus, no longer making enthusiastic plans for yourselves or your future. Communication problems are a thorn in any relationship – one of the most common reasons it starts to unravel. So start talking – and listening.

TIP: Ask your partner a decent question beyond what you would normally cover. Put some thought into it before you go out (there are lots of these date-sparkers on the internet). See what comes to you. And follow up on their answer!

4. The what-was-that-again test

You tell your partner a story or some news, or you update them on your day/life. Then you have to repeat yourself because they didn't hear you – their mind is somewhere else. Or perhaps you're the one who looks at them blankly? Everyone gets distracted from time to time but, if it's a repeat pattern, it gets boring – and it's dangerous for your relationship. We all want to feel heard and be understood by our partners – and none of us wants to feel boring.

TIP: Try not to multi-task when your partner's talking. Look at them. Respond to their statements (to show you've heard and stay focused). If you really struggle with distraction, bring yourself back by locking in on a colour or item of clothing they're wearing (don't say this out loud or do it too intensely – you'll be sprung).

5. The my-phone-is-more-interesting test

One (or both) of you is always on your phone or device. You tell yourself it's entertaining, it's useful, it's a time-filler, it's a distraction from the daily grind. Honestly, it gives you more than your partner does ... hmmm, there's a warning bell clanging.

TIP: Set (agreed) boundaries around your use of devices. Even a couple of e-free hours in the evening is a good start. Reward yourselves for sticking to it.

6. The niggle test

You find yourself picking fights over things you later realise are trivial. Be careful. Conflict is okay if the reason is fair and you can address it in a healthy way. If your niggling leads you to rip open old wounds, you're heading for trouble. It's not fair, either.

*TIP: Keep your criticisms current and specific – avoid attacking personal things that are difficult (if not impossible) to alter, such as your partner's genetics, intelligence, fears, weight or body shape. If you take a shot at who someone is, you'll hurt them deeply and you risk wounding your relationship beyond repair. People can accept they need to change their **behaviour**, but the idea of trying to change **who they are** will make them feel hopeless.*

7. The not-in-front-of-the-kids test

You usually keep your battles away from the kids but, one night, things spill over and they hear it all. You feel bad because you know it's not good for them. But you know stony silences aren't good either. You're right on both counts. Research tells us that kids take a psychological hit from both unresolved conflict and silence.

TIP: It can be healthy to raise issues in front of the kids so they can see it's okay to disagree. But you're also modelling your ability to manage conflict so, if your emotional management and conflict skills aren't sound, make it a priority to learn some.

8. The lonely-in-a-crowd test

You feel alone even when you're together. You don't feel your partner has got your back; you're not sure you're up for protecting theirs. You don't laugh and have fun together. You can't feel the connection anymore.

TIP: We're treading serious turf now, so sit down and talk honestly to your partner. Is it possible they feel it, too? Make a joint plan to address it. Avoiding problems can take you into a darker place, so speak up.

How to find fault 'nicely' (or the rules of healthy conflict)

How do you find fault with your partner?

Are you a nit-picker, yeller, nagger, martyr or 'dog with a bone'? If you are one of these, is it because you wouldn't need to be like that if they BLOODY HEARD YOU THE FIRST TIME?

Look, our partners annoy us. *Crumbs on the bench. Forgetting to put the rubbish out. Playing their music too loud. Dropping their stuff all over the house. Flinging clothes on the bedroom floor. Not getting the laundry in when it's raining. Buying new couch cushions when you already have 15. Toilet seat issues.*

We need to point those things out. But we also need to check in on our delivery: is it fair, well-timed and reasonable? (Note: Delivering king hits in a low, soothing voice does not mean you're reasonable; it may mean you're passive-aggressive.) People who are constantly under the hammer at home can become secretive, insecure, low in mood, lack confidence, angry and anxious. And, over time (even if they do what you say), they won't like you.

Here are some tips for delivering the nasty stuff nicely (because it's way cooler than being mean). They also serve as general rules for going into healthy battle in your relationship.

1. Check yourself first.

How we treat our partners is a reflection of who we are and where we're at. This can be hard to acknowledge – but it's important to do so. Your partner should be up for understanding your work stress, anxieties, life demands, quirks and whatever else is going on for you – but they shouldn't have to wear it, especially not on a daily basis. Before you find fault, check in with yourself. Take an inventory of your stress levels. It's possible that your arguments have less to do with your relationship and more to do with other stressors. Don't let Tony-from-work come between you. Because Tony-from-work won't care.

If you find yourself on the attack because you're tired and stressed, apologise, then take some time out. (Note: 'This is *just who I am*' is a poor excuse for bad behaviour.)

2. Know your own hot buttons.

Does an unmade bed drive you wild? Wet towels on the bedroom floor? Do you have a dirty socks and undies phobia? Do you flip out when feeling taken for granted? Seeing your partner chilling on the couch with mess all around? Angry you're doing too much? Guilty you're not doing more?

We all have multiple hot buttons. Knowing yours – those things that are sure to ignite a reaction in you – gives you some command over your behaviour. You'll be able to explain what's going on to your partner, before you enter the explosion zone. Speak up, rather than let your anger simmer to boiling point. Explosions can work if they're rare but, mostly, they just make things worse.

3. Check your standards.

In relationships, it's rare to have two partners with exactly the same standards – although wouldn't it be relaxing if we did? I worked with a man who was up scrubbing the pots almost before his partner had finished eating. It made meal times angsty and led to conflict. 'I know it's too much,' he said. 'I just can't sit still when there's work to be done.' It was positive that he knew it. His mission was to learn to let some things go. Check in on your expectations – make sure they are fair for both of you, not just what you need to settle your own anxiety.

4. Don't drip-feed criticisms.

Do not trickle criticisms through the day (and night). If you have a problem with your partner, set a time to sit down and discuss it. Not a whole evening, either. And not all your grievances all at once. Often, we pick at our partner over anything because we're feeling irritable, worried or distressed. But that's not a good time to start a 'discussion' – more likely, it will end in anger and/or tears. So pick your battles carefully and wait until you're in a good, or at least calmer, space.

5. Stay in the present (or else).

This might be the cardinal rule of all conflict. When something annoys or 'tips' you, it's tempting to drag up all the things that have annoyed you EVER. Big mistake. It sends a message to your partner that you don't like anything about them AND you've been storing up all this dislike for years! If you're mad about your partner's failure to do the dishes tonight, stay with the dishes. Stay with tonight. Don't hook every misdemeanour to past events. That's asking for trouble that never ends.

6. Praise more than condemn.

Check the balance between how much you praise and how much you find fault. It should weigh heavily in favour of appreciation. Sometimes, our frustrations can cause us to resent offering praise, even when it's due. If you're a Scrooge with praise, you need to tip the balance. Beginning now.

7. Be polite in your language.

Say 'please' and 'thank you', every time and more than you need to. People love to be thanked (because it equals feeling appreciated) – as long as it's genuine and sarcasm-free. It creates massive goodwill in a relationship.

8. Your partner is a person.

A person deserves to be treated like a person. If you can manage your emotions and behaviour out in the world, you can also do it at home. Treat your partner as you would a close friend, that's the least they deserve. (Warning: If you yell and rant at your friends, then your partner might be in trouble.)

9. Fight from a kind foundation.

Good partners keep the end game in mind. Things may get heated at times but their fights are underpinned by kindness and, even when they're locked in battle, they know they want to be together.

Remember, no-one is perfect and it's possible your partner may have a high annoyance factor. But how you find fault (and how much) often reflects your own character and the space you are in. Take aim if you must, but check in on yourself first.

Seven things you should never blame on your partner

Struggling relationships often slip into a blame-game: *he said* versus *she said* or *it's not my fault, it's yours*. And it's true that we tend to take out our negative feelings on those closest to us – which isn't always fair.

There are many things that can go awry in a relationship; many things you can peg on the troubles between the two of you. But these things are not them. These are things you have to own.

1. Your family and history

Perhaps you had a hypercritical parent? Perhaps you have low self-belief? Perhaps you've suffered trauma? Or never felt good enough for anyone? Those things may be valid, depending on your history, but that's no reason to flare up at your partner at the tiniest provocation. Be mad at your mother or father if you must, but leave your partner alone.

2. Your life choices

I worked with a man who resented his life choices – his career, the friends he'd made, the long list of things he hadn't done. His wife was on the list, too, but she was taking the blame for *all* of it.

The life you've chosen to lead can't be dumped all on your partner. Accept your own choices to date and know you can do many things differently from now on – and it's okay to ask for help to do so.

3. Your struggle to manage yourself

Regulating your moods, anxiety, anger, voice and physicality is an inside job – each of us has to do this for ourselves. While it's true that a difficult relationship can provoke us into uncharacteristic or dysfunctional behaviour, we need to own our actions. We all need to work continually on our emotional management skills. Above all, when you can't control yourself, don't target your partner. That's abuse.

4. Your job (and the people in it)

If you hate your job or boss, it's not your partner's fault (unless they're your boss). You're allowed to express your grumblings, but you're not allowed to dwell endlessly on them. Your partner doesn't want to talk through your office politics night after night. Your partner doesn't want to spend their evenings hearing about Ronnie or Lisa from work. You'll run their supportiveness dry. If you honestly can't find a way to improve your job, start looking for a new one – preferably today.

5. Your health – physical and mental

Okay, it's not helpful if your partner is a 'feeder' when you're trying to eat less and more healthily, or won't join you on weekend walks, or doesn't understand your anxiety. Hopefully, your partner is supportive of your health struggles and goals, but your health is your responsibility – ultimately, it's on you.

6. Your addictions

Alcohol, drugs, gambling, porn, food, work, shopping or anything else that has you nailed up against a wall. These issues are yours.

If you're lucky enough to have a loving partner, they'll support you while you work on them. If you stay in denial or refuse to work on them, don't expect your partner to stay. Not happily, anyway.

7. Your dissatisfaction with life

So you're unhappy? Identify and unpack the true reason for your misery. Is it really all about your relationship or love life? Often, it's not – it's only part of the package. It's okay to despise where you're at in life (because it can be a catalyst for change), but you need to know constant misery is hard to live with. Maybe you need to change your job, or eliminate a bad habit, or move away from a group of friends, or try a new activity or get more creative? There are lots of little things you can do to make yourself feel better. Pick one and start today – for everyone's sake.

Healthy conflict: Quick takeaways

- Disagreement can enhance intimacy. But regularly having sex after a fight is a bad idea.
- Constant fighting is hard on your mental health and relationship – and the kids.
- You are someone's role model: Your kids will watch you – and often copy.
- What happens between fights is a bigger deal than the fight itself. Check the general atmosphere between you. A good or content vibe matters most.
- It's hard to fight when you're sitting down. Even harder when you're holding hands.
- Blaming your partner for everything about your life is wrong – and mean.
- Wanting your relationship to work hugely influences your satisfaction in love – especially when you both do.

PART 2: TOXIC CONFLICT

'How starved you must have been that my heart became a meal for your ego.'

– Writer Amanda Torroni

Why does it matter? Toxic conflict is the dark, unhealthy side of love. Being a good partner includes establishing and maintaining healthy boundaries; knowing what you will and won't accept from the other person; and where necessary, keeping yourself physically, sexually and emotionally safe. In a troubled relationship, it can be hard to know when the conflict has become harmful – and when you should look for the exit door. This section aims to help.

A poisonous kind of love

We've established all relationships have issues – even those that are solid and loving. In a healthy relationship, conflict comes from a base of goodwill, support and affection (at least, most of the time), and wanting things to work out. In other words, there is calm and warmth between storms, along with a genuine desire to be together.

In a toxic relationship, there may be passion, but support, affection and genuine love are missing. The conflict and behaviours within the relationship are harmful in a pervasive, insidious way. While they may retreat at times, they never fully go away.

Although toxic relationships can come in many disguises, generally, they start out in one of two ways.

- The first – and the one that gets all the attention – is when one partner intentionally seeks to hurt, manipulate or control the unsuspecting other, either in obvious or subtle ways.

- The second is when the conflict between partners becomes so entrenched it poisons the relationship. Both partners develop dysfunctional ways of interacting/ behaving that hurt the other, and are difficult to recover from.

Toxic relationships can be abusive physically, sexually and/or psychologically/emotionally. The vast – and hugely important – realm of physical and sexual domestic violence is beyond the scope of this book. Emotional (or psychological) abuse, however, needs to be flagged as a hefty, and often stealthy, contributor to toxic relationships – and the hardest to detect. Many people suffer because they don't recognise the signs of emotional abuse, or it beds in so slowly they only register the severity of the problem when their health and wellbeing starts to suffer. As one woman said, 'I was in the car, listening to a radio interview with a woman who'd been psychologically abused by her partner. Suddenly, it hit me – I pulled over and burst into tears because I realised I'd been in an abusive relationship for years.'

Here are some tools to help identify the signs of emotional abuse, understand what's going on, and learn how to deal with and recover from it.

Psychological or emotional abuse

Psychological or emotional abuse is a common, and often quiet, form of relationship conflict. Things just happen, then keep happening, and while you know something's 'not right', it can be years until the abuse is acknowledged and you make moves to leave.

Emotional abuse is love with an agenda. Which isn't really love at all. It's when one partner seeks to control, discredit, isolate, confuse or scare the other. It may come in the form of criticism or threats or behaviour, which may cause you to doubt your perceptions and your reality. Sometimes, there's a pattern to it but, often, its sheer unpredictability is what makes it so hard to spot.

Even people who are aware of the signs may play them down because, in the eyes of society, emotional abuse is 'not as bad' as physical violence.

Hold on, though.

Just because emotional abuse won't put you in hospital with a broken bone, or threaten your safety/life, doesn't mean it's not destructive. Linked with anxiety, depression, trauma, low confidence or self-esteem, addictive behaviours, and physical health problems, emotional abuse can also impede your ability to parent, work and form healthy relationships. It can also escalate into physical or sexual violence, which is another compelling reason for not sweeping it under the carpet.

It's difficult to make generalisations about abusive relationships, because relationship dynamics are so complex and the types of abuse so varied. Based on research, case studies and the people I have worked with, however, the unpredictability, confusion and cumulative impact on a person's psyche can make it very difficult to break away.

Here are some signs you could be in an emotionally abusive relationship. Emotional abuse is not a classified disorder, so this list is not diagnostic in the official sense, nor is it exhaustive. If clusters of these signs are consistently showing up in your relationship, however, you should seek further advice.

You tiptoe around your partner.

You're never sure of their moods, and they can switch so suddenly from warm and fun to cold and distant. When they're in a good mood you can relax – but never entirely, because you never know when the next storm might blow in. And the storm is scary, or exhausting.

You say 'I'm sorry' excessively.

Sometimes, you're not sure what you did wrong, but you apologise anyway – it's easier to keep the peace. Take extra note if you do this more than you used to in previous relationships or in life generally.

You're reluctant to call out your partner.

Even when what you have to say is valid, you tend to clam up. Your partner will cleverly twist the circumstances to put the blame on you so then you doubt yourself: *'Was I wrong for raising this?'*

You're frequently told you 'overreact'.

When you're not overreacting. Or you don't think you are … but maybe you could be. It's happened so often that you get confused, you struggle to tell the difference.

Your partner brushes off their own poor behaviour.

This is designed to make you think you're overreacting. For example: *'It was just a bit of fun. Time got away on me. You know what I'm like when I'm with my work colleagues. You're making too much of this. Ha-ha! No big deal.'*

Your partner uses put-downs or ignores you.

You try to ignore the obvious degrading comments but even the subtle slights undermine your confidence. Your partner doesn't ignore you every time – sometimes they're lovely to you – but that's the point. You. Don't. Know. When. It's. Coming.

You've lost confidence generally.

You often second-guess your own thoughts and actions. You don't feel as confident in other areas of your life as you used to. You feel like your sense of self has been diminished.

You find yourself excusing your partner's poor behaviour.

You wonder if they're depressed, or have a personality disorder, or are the product of a difficult family background. These things may be true, but that doesn't give them a leave pass to treat you poorly, especially when it keeps happening over a long time. You still have to consider what it's like for YOU to be in a relationship with them.

Your partner often changes plans on you (and others).

These changes come suddenly and will be spun to look like it's fun/exciting/better for you – but in reality, it's anxiety-provoking. It's also a means of controlling you, of keeping you standing on shifting sand, so you can't make definite plans of your own.

Your partner is secretive.

Your partner is very protective of their phone. They'll disappear without telling you where they're going. And when they go out/ away, you're never entirely sure what they're doing (and who they're with).

Your partner is investigative.

While they don't want you to know what *they're* doing, they'll want to know the finer details of what *you're* up to, who you're with and what time you'll be home. It's feels like more than interest, it's an investigation.

You're not sure what's normal in a relationship.

You're not happy and relaxed in your relationship; you have a feeling that the erratic way your partner treats you isn't right, but you don't know what goes on for other couples. Maybe this is normal? You feel driven to seek outside advice.

You keep telling yourself you love them.

And you probably do. But loving someone doesn't mean it's okay for them to treat you badly. Loving someone doesn't mean you have to stay with them at all costs. And loving someone doesn't make them, or turn them into, a good partner.

So, is it okay?

Difficulties occur in all relationships, mostly without lasting damage. But if there are clusters of traits – if you find yourself nodding to several of these signs, then it's likely you're in an unhealthy, possibly abusive, relationship.

If it's been going on for a while, or if you're inexperienced in relationships, you may have started to accommodate your partner's behaviours. That can make it hard to tell what's within the *normal and acceptable range* of relationship behaviour.

If you're concerned, write down some examples and get an outside view. Also check in on your own mental health, particularly noting if there's been a decline related to your relationship. Your partner should never have the power to rob you of your wellbeing.

Mind games: Are you being played?

Do you feel something's 'off' in your relationship? That you're being controlled, or pressured to do things you don't want to do, or to do them in a certain way? Or you're doubting and questioning yourself a lot more than you used to? Chances are someone is pulling your strings – and not with good intent, either.

Psychological manipulation can occur in any close relationship – it's most common in intimate relationships, between partners or, to a lesser degree, with parents. But it can also occur at work, where one person has (or seeks) power over another.

If you feel uneasy about a relationship, it's important to understand its dynamics, so you can navigate it and, if necessary, protect yourself.

Psychological manipulation in a relationship is controlled through mind games. There's a secondary goal, too: to undermine, confuse and bring down the targeted person.

These tactics sit at the core of bullying behaviour – and emotionally abusive relationships. The signs can be subtle, they come and go, and the people who use them are skilled at it.

There are many ways you can be manipulated. The following list includes the 'best' of what I've seen in my therapy work. I call them the seven deadly sins of manipulation.

1. Information gathering: Wanting to know ALL about you

Manipulators often start out with flattery. They'll show lots of interest in you, and ask lots of questions – some light, some deep and probing. You'll find yourself opening up because they make you feel interesting, even fascinating.

Yes, this can also be the hallmark of a socially skilled person. But a manipulator's questions *have an agenda*. They're gathering up all your insecurities and vulnerabilities – not to support you, but to use them against you when it suits them. This often takes the form of controlling you in the relationship or getting back at you after it's over.

2. Inconsistency: Keeping you guessing

The game is to keep you on shaky ground: to lift you up, then dump you down. Rinse and repeat. So you're never sure when you're in favour with your partner – or not.

You'll be criticised or treated badly, then given an extravagant birthday present (which they'll want you to tell other people about). It's not because they're generous or want to make up; it's to confuse you. *What's going on? Are they good or bad? Do they love me or not?*

3. Guilt-tripping: Making you prove your love

This is when you're coerced into proving your love or devotion by doing things for them, such as chores or special favours. The manipulator often takes the victim role, making you seem like the bully or assailant.

You'll hear lines like: *'How could you do that to me?'* or *'If you really loved me, you would ...'* or *'You could prove your love by ....'*

4. Blaming: Implying their wrongs are YOUR fault

When you protest against a hurtful or stinging comment, a manipulator will indicate that you're too sensitive, overreacting, or you've lost your sense of humour. *'Wow, someone got out of bed on the wrong side today. It was only a joke. I didn't think you'd take it that way. Calm down. You're making way too much of this.'*

This is intended to cause you to doubt your reactions, to wonder if you really are making too much of a fuss. It's confusing: You lose your emotional radar as to which comments or actions need or deserve a reaction. And you lose your ability to judge the emotional intensity required.

5. Personal attack: Targeting things you can't change

The best manipulators will keep you on a leash (and your anxiety humming) with a series of low-level jabs. But when they want to take it up a notch, they'll go after your personality, your inbuilt, rather than learned, traits. *'You're not very good with people. You do tend to get upset easily. You don't handle pressure/ deadlines well. You're just not a social person. You're too anxious to attempt that/take that on.'*

Note: This is intriguing because whatever aspect of you the manipulator targets is often a projection of their own insecurity.

6. Silent treatment: Making you guess what's going on

A classic control tactic. The silent treatment, ignoring or withdrawal aims to increase your anxiety over whatever it is you're supposed to have done wrong, so you become almost desperate for a reaction, or explanation, from them.

They'll vary the time of each 'withdrawal', so you'll never know how long they'll take to come out of it. In the workplace, a manipulative boss will tend to give you little attention or cancel meetings with you (then reschedule them for when they know it doesn't suit you), or pretend they're super-busy. Then they'll emerge as though nothing ever happened – so you'll look foolish if you raise it.

7. Gaslighting: Forcing you to question your sanity

Gaslighting is the oldest trick in the manipulation handbook. It takes its name from the 1938 British play *Gas Light*, in which an abusive husband manipulates his wife to make her think she's gone mad.

A 'gaslighter' methodically sows the seeds of doubt, causing their target to question themselves and their reality: their memory, perception and judgement. *'Did I imagine it? Am I overreacting? Am I the troubled one? Am I losing my mind?'*

It can start small but, over time, gaslighting can severely erode your ability to navigate daily life.

What can you do?

If you find yourself in a relationship with someone who uses these tactics, wise up. If you're exposed to them for a long time, you'll pay a hefty psychological price. Here are some strategies to help.

It's not you.

Gather evidence about their treatment of you – write it down and date it while you can remember it. This will provide you with evidence that you're not imagining or exaggerating it (as a manipulative partner will want you to think). When you're ready, you can use this to seek outside validation for your situation, that you are not dreaming it or to blame for it.

Don't expect an apology or change in behaviour.
Because you won't get it. Or, if you do, it won't be genuine. It will likely be something they do to get the next thing they want.

Don't try to play them at their own game.
They will win. They've likely been doing this a long time. They may have been honing their tactics since childhood, then using them on others, so they are good – very good.

Set boundaries for your health and safety.
Boundaries and hard lines are important, especially if you need to maintain the relationship for family or other reasons. The very first boundary you should set is time for yourself. You also need to be able to say 'no' clearly to any requests you don't have the time/energy for or you're not okay with. Beyond setting boundaries, you may need coaching from a trusted party to stick to them.

Sometimes, the best strategy is the exit door.
You may know this yourself. If you're confused, seek outside or professional help with making a decision and plan. Don't let things drag on too long because you're compromising your health, identity and future.

Know that things will get better.
This is what you have to hang on to as you seek to change your situation. It's not easy, but it's true. Life on the other side can be good, better, even truly great. Aim for greener grass ahead.

How to tell if there's a narcissist in your bed

Narcissism is a cluster of disordered personality traits that fall under the toxic relationship umbrella. I've included it as its own section because the topic of 'narcissistic partners' comes up so frequently in therapy – usually raised by people hurting in the wake of a breakup.

Narcissism – or Narcissistic Personality Disorder (NPD) – is a classified mental health condition characterised by an extreme self-focus, a deep need for admiration and a lack of empathy for others' feelings. Beneath that veneer is a brittle self-esteem, and a vulnerability to even minor slights and criticism.

Like many psychologists, I'm careful about diagnosing NPD, and wouldn't do it from a person's second-hand report of their partner. Personality disorders are hefty labels and the condition isn't black and white. Narcissism sits on a scale from mild to severe; it is estimated that less than 1 per cent of people meet the criteria at its most extreme. It's also important to note that a degree of narcissism can show up in healthy individuals as confidence or good self-esteem.

In unpacking toxic relationships, however, it's useful to consider the key traits of narcissism. Remember, one or two of these signs don't point to a diagnosis of NPD. But when clusters of these traits show up consistently, it's time to take notice – or at least get a neutral/professional view of what might be going on.

Narcissism: A psychology checklist for understanding a partner*

1. You'll feel loved like you've never been loved.
At first, narcissists act like you're a drug to them. They'll shower you with love and attention in ways that are addictive. Many

* Adapted from the *Diagnostic and Statistical Manual of Mental Disorders* (DSM-5) and acknowledging the diagnostic approach to personality disorder assessment offered by the International Classification of Diseases ICD-11, along with other reading.

people mistake this for true love, or believe they've found their soulmate. The trouble with this attention is that it's not real – they are simply mirroring all your best qualities back to you. It's seductive; there's no feeling quite like it – until they decide you're NOT the perfect person after all. Which, at some point, they will.

2. They see the world through a single lens – theirs.

This spells trouble in a relationship because when you have a disagreement (or even when you don't), a narcissistic partner will find it *impossible* to see your point of view. It's not because they don't want to – they just can't.

I once witnessed a man whose partner had admitted cheating on him – twice. Even though she could see his devastation (tears), and an apology was the easiest (and right) thing to do, she was fixed on justifying her behaviour. I felt extremely worried for my client because I could see the pain he'd signed on for. It took him a long time to get out of the relationship and to recover from it.

3. They can't make a genuine apology.

Even when a narcissist says 'Sorry', they won't mean it. That's because they can't see they were wrong.

4. Their emotional intelligence is child-like.

Although narcissists can be extremely intelligent, their ability to process and express genuine emotion (that's appropriate for the occasion) is stunted, like that of a child. This can usually be tracked back to how they were raised; for example, by neglectful, over-indulgent or enmeshed parents.

This doesn't mean they're not emotional – they are often wildly so – but when you analyse it, you'll see their emotional responses don't fit, or match, the occasion. It's too much, or too little, or just plain impossible to understand.

5. They don't like you being upset.

Because they're uncomfortable with any emotion other than their own, they get squirmy with your distress – they don't know what to do with it. Lack of empathy is one of the hallmark features of narcissism – but in a relationship, it goes further than that. It *disappoints* them to see you upset, or vulnerable, because it means you aren't the 'ideal' person they thought you were. You fall from the pedestal they've put you on – and this is when they begin to devalue you. Which, sadly, is inevitable.

6. You'll never be able to give them enough attention.

Because no-one can. Life with a narcissist is a constant round of trying to make them feel as superior and wonderful as the false impression they have of themselves suggests.

7. They use control tactics to make you doubt your sanity.

Two of the common control tactics you won't find on narcissism checklists are (1) sleep deprivation, and (2) raising your mental health issues. Sleep deprivation is subtle. Narcissists may wake their partners at random times to 'chat', but ensure that the talk is in some way upsetting or unsettling, and leaves them unable to sleep. Mental health issues, such as '*Oh, I see your anxiety is back again*' or '*Given your mental health issues, you would see it that way*', are raised to undermine your judgement and yourself.

8. They strike deals.

They can be generous, especially if they have money, but they'll never do something nice for you without there being a kickback. They'll keep score. They'll withhold money or attention or sex or love on a whim, all of which are ways of controlling the relationship – and you.

9. They have few (if any) long-term friends.

They're often charming and appear to make friends easily, but their friendships don't go the distance. When they perceive that someone has let them down, they find it easy to cut them loose and never look back. You may find a few old friends in their distant past but, even then, there will have been frequent fallouts. Look closely and you'll see a hot–cold pattern in their friendships and family relationships.

10. You'll begin to feel emotionally exhausted.

The silences, the gaslighting (where everything is turned around to be your fault), the deal-striking, the criticisms and nit-picking, the emotional rollercoaster, and the unpredictability of their moods and love, is exhausting. Over time, it gets worse. One day, you'll wake up depleted, knowing you barely have the energy to do what you need to do – end the relationship.

11. You won't feel solid in the relationship – or in anything.

You'll no longer feel grounded AND you'll begin to lose your sense of who you are. You'll develop an underlying anxiety from never knowing what to expect and being unable to relax until you know your partner is in a good space.

You'll lose yourself. Your boundaries or idea of what's acceptable in a healthy relationship will shift and, slowly, you'll shape yourself to accommodate the personality, and demands, of your partner. You'll feel like it's not right, but you're not sure – because sometimes it is. And that usually means you stay, until you get forced out.

What it means

Again, this is not a diagnostic tool, it's a checklist to help you unpack your difficult relationship. It should also be considered on a scale, ranging from mild to severe. But you don't need a diagnosis to ask the one crucial question of yourself: *Are you thriving in your relationship – or not? Because you should be and deserve to be.*

It's not you, it's them

Being in a toxic relationship can wreak such emotional havoc, you slowly lose sight of who you are. It can make you behave strangely – even badly, turning you into someone you barely recognise.

I've seen both men and women struggling in the wake of toxic or abusive relationships, and they often have a nagging doubt about their own role. *Do I have narcissistic traits, too?* It's a common question when a relationship has turned you upside down; it's hard to figure out where the line begins and ends. If you're with, or have been with such a person, here's some quick reassurance that *it wasn't you, it was them.*

1. You want to educate yourself about relationships.

After your breakup, you jump online, dive into the literature, and ask questions of people who know more than you. You want to know what happened. You want to understand your ex-partner's operating system and how something that started so well could turn so bad. You want to figure out what's going on for you now – why you feel so exhausted and broken by them. A narcissist won't educate themselves, because they'll think they did nothing wrong – that the problem was with you. That they're fine and you're the one who needs fixing.

2. You're up for seeing a therapist if you need more help.

If you're really struggling, you'll reach out for help. A narcissist won't – or they might start going to therapy all bright and shiny but, after a while, the therapist won't be good/intelligent/ understanding enough for them. Or, as soon as they sense the therapist can see behind their mask, they'll be off and running.

3. You don't have a string of broken relationships behind you.

Depending on your age and stage, you might have a few relationships that haven't worked out. But narcissists keep up the pattern – often right through until old age. Because they can't (and have never been able to) love, and they need constant adoration/validation; they can't sustain intimate relationships. You'll often see this pattern repeated in their friendships and work. They'll bubble and charm for a while – but they can't keep it up. They'll often bolt before they're found out.

4. You'll struggle with anxiety/self-doubt after the breakup.

Intense or difficult breakups can leave people with low mood; anxiety; and trauma symptoms such as hypervigilance, flashbacks, panic and paranoia. You can become extremely fearful at the prospect of bumping into your ex again. Even a sighting of them on social media can distress you. It's also common to second-guess your role in the relationship, worry about what you did wrong and doubt your attractiveness as a partner. You need to address these things so they don't get in the way of you loving again.

While narcissists are deeply insecure at their core, they'll generally feel only one of two emotions after a breakup: a false happiness, because they've moved on to someone else, or anger if you're the one who ended it. When their egos get bruised, narcissists can become fixated on payback or smear campaigns. So if you're the one who called time, go quietly and don't look back.

5. You're able to apologise genuinely.

In fact, if you've been with a narcissist, you've probably apologised far more than you need to – for little, if anything. You may have apologised just to keep the peace. Genuine apologies don't appear on the narcissist's song sheet. Even if they do manage a 'sorry' here and there, there'll be an agenda lurking.

6. You don't keep contacting your ex just to 'see how they're doing'.

When we break up with someone, most of us are prone to a little low-key stalking – until we see the light. But it's never over for the narcissist. They'll keep tabs on you any way they can. It's not that they still love you (they didn't, they can't), but they need to use you to validate themselves. They are driven to check they could still have you if they tried. And they might keep doing it for years after you've broken up. Hopefully, you know there's no gain in responding, unless you need to stay in contact because you have children together.

7. You're reading this!

Narcissists don't read about narcissism. Or healthy relationships. Are you kidding? They're (superficially) all good with who they are. And, of course, they have much better things to do – and way cooler people to play with.

Why it takes so long to leave a toxic relationship

> 'I have to remember it is not love that has hurt me; but someone who could not love me in the right way.'
>
> – Rebecca YS Perez

If you're in a difficult relationship, be gentle with yourself. Even when you know it's wrong, there can be significant barriers to leaving. It's common for people to be alert to difficulties early in toxic relationships, but it can take years to break free of them. Frequently, they'll make many attempts but, for complex reasons, they're drawn back. When they finally leave, there's bewilderment to go with the pain. *Why did I put up with so much crap? Why did I waste so much time? Why did I pour heart and soul into a person who almost broke me?*

The cycle of abuse has been used to describe the pattern of calm, tension, violence and reconciliation that occurs in abusive relationships.

As its critics have suggested, however, it's difficult to generalise, mostly because relationship dynamics are so complex and the types of abuse – such as psychological manipulation – are so varied.

Based on the people I have worked with, the enmeshed periods of calm and storm, and the cumulative impact on your psyche, can make it extremely difficult to break away.

I've seen all sorts of people get caught in these relationships but, more often, it's those who've come from a toxic history or have been with toxic partners previously, so believe them to be the 'norm', and those who have never experienced toxicity before, so they find it hard to believe it's happening.

Plenty of valid reasons (such as money, children, assets and pets) can keep people stuck in unhealthy relationships. Here are the main emotional reasons it can take so long to exit.

You're not experienced in (healthy) relationships.

We step into our first relationships as learners. We're uncertain of how to play it, so we get things muddled or wrong. Or we haven't yet had a 'healthy' relationship (or had one modelled to us), so we don't know what a good relationship looks like.

It takes time to learn and get good at anything, and the same holds true in relationships. Inexperience is a tripwire for even confident, well-balanced people, because a toxic partner will take advantage of them, with their full arsenal of manipulative tactics.

You don't believe it's happening.

Many people will report seeing red flags early in the relationship – some even within the first month. For example, an argument that blew in from nowhere or an unreasonably strong reaction to a minor event. But they brush it aside because: *All relationships have teething problems, right? It couldn't be that bad, could it?* Love, or even infatuation, has a nasty way of blinding us to the truth. When mixed with inexperience, it's a recipe for trouble.

You want to help this person.

Your partner has difficulties – you know that. But something (good) in you wants to help make it right. You can see all their great qualities; they have so much potential; and if you just give them the support they need (or have never had), you'll have a winner. He/she is worth it so you keep trying, beyond the call of duty, even when it taxes your own wellbeing.

Your partner is a master manipulator.

Toxic partners are superb at what they do. That's because their interactive styles originated in childhood and they've been practising them ever since. Don't think you'll be a match for a master manipulator – you won't be. They will play you until you question your sanity. If you try to leave, they'll turn on the charm until you take them back. And then you'll be back where you started.

Your partner has done a hatchet job on your self-esteem.

Maybe your self-esteem was low before you got into the relationship, so your partner went after your vulnerability? But it's not always the case. Sometimes, people go into such relationships with solid, even high, levels of self-worth – only to have them systematically chipped away.

Interestingly, it can sometimes take a confident, secure person even longer to see, or face, the problems because they don't believe it's happening to them.

You are ashamed of your relationship (and your place in it).
People in toxic relationships are often skilled secret-keepers. They keep the true nature of the relationship hidden, because they don't want others to think badly of their partner and they want to protect their own reputation. It's hard to admit you've made a mistake in making such an important choice – a partner.

You need time to build courage and make a plan.
You really do. It takes courage. Resolve. Support. And you need the logistics in place: a place to live and the financial means to support yourself and any children. You may need a job – or a better one than you currently have. This can be a huge hurdle for people wanting to leave.

If you have managed to leave, be compassionate with yourself. It takes time to recover, to heal. Just know that you will.

The other side: What a toxic relationship can teach you – but only when you're ready

> 'Letting go means to come to the realization that some people are a part of your history, but not a part of your destiny.'
>
> – Steve Maraboli

It's over: You're free of your toxic relationship
You know your partner was bad for you. You know you're in a (way) better place now. And yet, it doesn't feel as good as it should.

You're still wrestling with anxiety, sadness, shame and anger. Some nights, after a drink or three, you still find your fingers hovering over your phone, wanting to text them.

Welcome to the relationship recovery room. It's a hard place to land. Toxic relationships can trigger feelings of unworthiness, helplessness, fear, anxiety, depression, insecurity, paranoia and shame. And, if it's your first experience of toxicity, it strips you of your innocence. It can leave you cynical and fearful of love.

Those scars can, and will, heal. Because when (and only when) you're ready, you'll dive into educating yourself about what happened. And the things you learn will help you love again.

You learn red flags are subtle.

Advice often touts you'll come out of a toxic relationship knowing all the red flags, so you'll never make that mistake again. I'm not sure who's giving that advice but it's dumb, wrong – and even a little mean. Red flags are not blindingly obvious in a new relationship. That's because toxic people are highly skilled at hiding their flaws. And because when we meet someone new, we're looking for the good in them. We're not (and shouldn't be) trying to spot all the reasons we shouldn't be there!

So the best advice is to take your time before you commit. A person always reveals themselves and, after a while, the truly toxic just can't help it.

You learn how you want to be treated.

Not. Like. That. Right?

You learn how a toxic relationship affects people.

'You don't know how tough a situation can be until you've been there.' This old saying is so true in the case of toxic relationships. Even many of your friends won't fully understand what you've been through. People who haven't been there won't 'get' the bone-rattling anxiety; deep sadness; flashes of anger; guilt and shame; pain; and the big, crazy emotional rollercoaster ride you're on or have been on. But here's the thing: your experience will make you deeply empathetic to others going through a similar situation, and that's a good thing.

You learn how being with a toxic partner can change you.

One of the frightening things about being with a toxic partner is how they change you. How they goad you into becoming a person you don't recognise and, at times, don't like. All those fights? All those nasty verbals? Well, you had to lash back, didn't you? It changed you, and not in a good way. You'll never want to sacrifice Who You Are like that again.

You learn people become more of who they are – not less.

It's a universal truth that our best and worst traits exaggerate over time. People change, and our circumstances change, but most of us don't change at our core. So, that tiny flash of utterly irrational anger you spotted on your second date? That nasty comment made under their breath about an innocent person in the street? That smart-arse attitude in a restaurant? You've since found out there was a whole lot more where that came from.

You learn that no relationship is better than a harmful one.

People often enter into (and stay in) unhealthy relationships because they're scared of being alone. Being alone is tough if it's not your choice, but you're never going to harm yourself in the way a toxic partner will – not even close. More than one client in a terrible relationship has told me: 'Better the devil you know … right?' Er, no. Horribly wrong. Why would you partner with the devil?

You learn ALL about boundaries.

Toxic partners jump all over your boundaries, back and forth – it's part of the game to confuse and keep you guessing. You want a night at home? Forget it. Your partner NEEDS to see you. You want to see your own friends? Nope. Your Favourite Person wants to see you more. You want to be with your partner? Suddenly, they don't want to see you, they have lots of other things to do.

Gradually, you lose your way. Your toxic partner is pulling all your strings. Boundaries are key in a healthy relationship: now you know that 100 per cent.

You learn what you don't (ever) want.

To be lied to, manipulated, controlled, criticised, gaslit? Made to feel like you're a lesser human being by someone who is a poor example of one? To feel fearful, pressured? To be almost begging to please someone, who is supposed to love and support you, but treats you with disdain? Yeah ... nah. Actually, NO THANKS. I'll pass on that.

You learn who the most important person in a relationship is.

Hopefully, this doesn't need any further explanation.

You learn how strong you are.

Truly. It takes a massive dose of inner strength to clear out on someone you truly loved – even when you know how much they hurt you. If you're on the other side of a toxic relationship and you're feeling okay, and determined to be better, you're the winner. Trust me.

Making your comeback: How to know you're on your way back

There's no timeframe for getting over any breakup – let alone a traumatic one. Beware of studies that put a precise number on it (*e.g. you'll be all good in 3 months and 16 days*), because healing is a process, not a statistic. If anyone tries to sell you on a timeframe, they probably have one eye on your wallet.

You'll have good days and bad, and when you have a setback, it can be hard to see any progress. But you will get there. Just know that every day out of a bad relationship is a triumph.

When you are on the comeback trail you will:

See the relationship for what it was.

You're not in denial; you've accepted it happened. It's not what you'd have chosen, and maybe it took you longer than you wanted to leave, but you're out. You won't go back, even if your ex begged you to try. You don't have to get to the point of loving or forgiving your ex, you just have to accept that being with them was part of your story.

Be taking good care of yourself.

Following a difficult breakup, people often neglect themselves. It's not intentional, but they can't think straight, or their emotions are so jagged, they can't stick to good routines. They may eat badly, drink too much or try to cope in ways they know are unhealthy. The mental stress may cause physical problems, too, such as unexplained aches and pains, colds and flu, headaches, and autoimmune difficulties. You know you're on the way back when you're trying to eat well, getting fresh air and exercise, taking care of your appearance, and nurturing your body.

No longer feel constant anxiety.

The dread that sat in your chest has begun to dissolve. You're able to hear the name of your ex – or see them in a social media post – without falling apart. At times, you're still anxious, but you feel like you can step out in the world without being flooded by emotions. You know it'll take time before the pain stops blowing in from left field. But most of the time, you can pick yourself up or calm yourself down as needed.

Have done your 'homework'.

You've researched and tried to understand the relationship you were in. You've taken time to educate yourself, on your own or through a therapist. You now know the key signs of toxicity. You understand your role, and know what you'd do differently next time. You know your dealbreakers, too; you're aware of what you will and won't tolerate in a future partner. You've also made an effort to know what 'healthy' and a 'good partner' mean to you. In other words, you're armed.

Have stopped beating up on yourself.

When emerging from a toxic relationship, guilt and shame are common emotions, along with the sheer frustration that you stayed in it so long. Maybe you didn't like the person you became in the relationship either. But you've realised that you were in a no-win situation; you've stopped blaming yourself for being with someone who was only ever going to hurt you. You're being good to yourself instead.

Feel like being with people.

That (natural and normal) need to hide from the world is beginning to retreat. At first, you had to force yourself to do things and see friends but, lately, you've started to feel a tiny beat of enthusiasm. You're beginning to say 'yes' to things beyond your immediate circle and you've stopped dreading going to them. Even if you can't quite face dating yet, you're open to new opportunities.

Be hopeful about your future.

You acknowledge the relationship (and exit) was extraordinarily difficult, but you no longer see it as life-limiting. You're starting to feel more like yourself and you're up for finding out more about who you are. You're lighter and more hopeful about what lies ahead. You know that, in your own time and in your own way, you'll be able to love again.

Toxic conflict: Quick takeaways

- Not all love is good for us – some is poisonous.
- Emotional scars can be as hurtful as physical ones.
- Toxic partners are good at what they do. Educate yourself.
- If you're reading this book, you're not a narcissist.
- A toxic relationship will hurt you, but it doesn't have to define you.
- You can recover if you take steps to do so and are patient with yourself.
- When you're ready, you will love again.

Can you be naked
(in every sense)?

'He showed me his scars, and in return he let me pretend
that I had none.'

– Madeline Miller

Why does it matter? Intimacy is the unique closeness you have
with your partner. It's that 'you and me against the world' feeling.
While intimacy is most commonly associated with sex and
physical touch, there are other types of intimacy. The key is being
able to be vulnerable and open with each other.

***

While I was writing this book, one of my clients asked me to name
the seven pillars. I reeled them off; he stopped me at Intimacy.
'That's the one I want to read,' he said. 'The one about sex.'

We laughed. I understood: sex is the sexy bit of relationships and, if you've just read the chapter on Conflict, you'll know it's also one of the main causes of trouble – from infidelity (or worries about it) right through to when should we, how should we, how often should we and 'if you don't mind I'd rather read a book'.

The other thing is that sex has played a massive trick on us, getting us all excited in the early stages of a relationship but not telling us things would change. I've often thought that sex should come with a warning sticker: 'Libido can fluctuate or even change markedly with time, hormones, kids, illness, surgery, mental health issues, age, life stressors and other variables.' The trouble for relationships is that some people's libido doesn't change at all. So, for a lot of couples, problems brew in the gap. Discrepancy in sexual desire is one of the biggest problems couples face.

By definition, intimacy is simply your closeness to people in personal relationships. It isn't, as is commonly believed, another word for sex. Nor is it a subset of sex. It's actually the other way round. You can have intimacy without sex, just as you can have sex without intimacy. For most couples, however, the two are (rightly or wrongly) perceived as a package deal and that's where things get all messed up.

In this chapter, we'll take a look at the four types of intimacy, how you see/rate intimacy in your relationship and the key struggles with intimacy. But first, an insider's look at secrets as being a big barrier to intimacy.

When secrets get in the way: Eli's story

Eli is keeping a secret from his partner, Seth. He says they're happy together. Sex is great, they communicate well and iron out disagreements quickly. It's easily the best relationship Eli has ever had and he wants it to last.

Suddenly, he stops mid-sentence and looks at me intently. 'But there's one big problem. He wants me to move in with him and I don't want to.'

'It's okay to take your time, isn't it? Is there any rush?' I ask.

'No. But I can **never** move in with him.' Again, that intensity. 'It's my eating,' he finally says, covering his face with his hands. 'I have a big problem.'

Eli had been an overweight teen and was extremely conscious of it, so he'd become a 'gym junkie'. His overweight days now well behind him, he's ripped and proud of his body. But he describes a pattern of binge eating that's increasingly difficult to hide from Seth – or from anyone. He'd binge for a day then either purge or punish himself by starving for a day. He'd hit the gym twice a day and smash his body with weights and cardio training. On the subject of food and exercise, he was off and running. He talked calories, kilocalories and kilojoules. He understood carbohydrates and lipids, fats, proteins and fibre. He knew the moisture content of foods. He knew the high-tech ways to burn fat. He constantly worked trade-offs in his head. *If I eat this, then I need to do that. And that. And that.*

Eli knew that if he moved in with Seth, he'd be sprung. 'Seth is completely normal around food. He has a burger and fries, and doesn't think twice – but one burger will cause me days of stress. The trouble is, he thinks I'm normal. He loves the way I look. What's he going to do when he finds out who I really am?'

I feel a surge of empathy. I've seen this problem before, where the stress of hiding a problem – with food (restricting or bingeing), alcohol, drugs, gambling or porn – becomes as big as the problem itself. I recall working with a man who couldn't figure out his partner's eating behaviour. She'd recently moved in, but wouldn't eat dinner with him. She made multiple excuses: the gym, her work, being out with friends. After three weeks, he was confused. Why was she never home for dinner? After six weeks, he was annoyed. Then she told him about her chronic eating struggles. For a long time, he was patient and supportive. But she wouldn't seek help. He kept dining alone. Eventually, they broke up.

I've had clients who had to live alone, not because they liked having their own space, but because they needed it. They could maintain a façade of normality at work and in many other situations, but behind the front door, dysfunction reigned. They were in the grip of issues that held the balance of power over them.

It's a difficult place. People with these struggles want to form loving relationships. But their secrets stop them from getting close to anyone. They keep up their guard to avoid intimacy. Being unable to be fully vulnerable is a barrier to intimacy. And, without intimacy, it's hard to be a good partner because you can't sustain a loving relationship.

The four types of intimacy

Another word for intimacy is vulnerability. It's being 'naked' with someone else, it's showing who you truly are. So it's not surprising that intimacy and sex are often lumped together under the same banner. Sex is seen as the ultimate 'closeness'; through the ages, it's been used to seal the deal on – or consummate – committed relationships and it's what makes your partner more than a great mate.

Certainly, sex can build intimacy in a relationship. But anyone who's been in a relationship for a while will tell you that you need more than sexual closeness to make it work. Having wild and wicked sex all day long doesn't stop the dishes mounting up. It doesn't pay the bills or take care of your life admin or feed the dog. After a hard day at the office with your boss from Hell, most aren't wanting to rush into the bedroom with their partner of 10 years while the kids get their own dinner. (Apologies if you do.)

Here's the point. While sex is an important component of a relationship, our intimate needs can be met in many ways. More than that, they need to be. If sex is all you have and want, all power to you. But most people want to feel loved and appreciated with their clothes on, too.

There are many different types of intimacy. Couples can bond through any activities they share: prayer or sports or food or music or books or boardgames or gaming or Netflix or their families. Anything, really. There are no ground rules about how you can be close – nor should there be. But true intimacy takes closeness up a notch, and for most people, these needs are covered in four ways. You don't need all four to have a good relationship, and you don't need all four at once and forever. But, if you're lucky (and you put the effort in), you'll get all of them to varying degrees throughout the course of your love.

After checking out the following intimacy quartet, use the exercise at the end to assess how you see intimacy.

1. Physical and sexual intimacy

Physical/sexual intimacy usually shows up first in a relationship. When we like someone, we touch them (well, perhaps not the second we first meet them, but when it's appropriate). Hand-holding, kissing, hugs and sex all meet the early goals for physical and sexual intimacy. At a certain point in a relationship, having (consensual) sex seems straightforward, but it can be a real struggle for some. Core beliefs about sex, such as those tied to religion, can get in the way of expressing your sexual self. Negative self-evaluations about bodies, weight, physical attractiveness and sexual performance can all be barriers to healthy sex. People often need a lot of reassurance to take off their clothes, let alone relax into and enjoy sex. While it's more common for women to feel physically insecure, men can also be anxious (e.g. resulting in erectile dysfunction) and transgender people can struggle hugely with the mismatch between their physical form and how they view themselves.

Body insecurity isn't just the domain of the young either. Bodies change and, with them, so can our confidence. Women often report a loss of body confidence after childbirth; even though their bodies have done their finest work, there can be sorrow at what's been lost. Ageing, too, takes its toll. A client in her late 50s, who'd been on her own for years, had met a man online who she liked. They were about to spend their first weekend together and she was petrified about getting naked in front of him. She returned with a positive report: 'It was okay,' she said, smiling. 'When I saw he wasn't stressed about having man boobs, I decided not to worry about my flabby bits either.'

Physical touch and sex are important in relationships, and the goal should be to find a place where you're both comfortable. Shutting down about discrepancies in desire, or just drifting apart, can lead to resentment and a loss of connection. I worked with a man whose partner didn't want sex after undergoing invasive surgery. It wasn't about not having sex or an orgasm: 'I can take care of myself,' he said. It was that he wanted to be understanding and loving towards his partner, but he wasn't sure how to express it.

'Not wanting sex doesn't mean she doesn't love you,' I said.

'She told me that.'

'Don't you believe her?'

'Yes, but ...' He frowned, suddenly looking terribly insecure. When he finally managed to speak, he said he didn't know how else to show her love, and he worried she'd lose interest in him. I felt sorry for him. His idea of intimacy was completely bound to sex, which is common for men. This can cause problems, especially when sexual desire wanes over time.

My client needed reassurance to understand his partner's love for him hadn't changed – but her body and sex drive had. There would be some adjustments to their previously healthy sex life. He also needed to reframe his idea of intimacy and to talk to his partner about what they *could* do, rather than what they couldn't.

Everyone has different intimate needs, but many – more often women – just want to be seen and heard, loved and valued, and made to feel special. That's a whole lot harder than just having sex.

Many couples experience sexual problems, but they can be difficult to speak about, which can build tension even between couples who love each other, so it's important these problems aren't tucked under the mattress, so to speak.

Keys to addressing sexual problems

- Don't take the difficulties personally – often, it's more about what's going on for your partner. Check in on what's happening in their life.
- Be gentle and reassuring about your love outside sex.
- Be patient. You don't have to 'fix' problems immediately; they don't have to dictate the future of your relationship. They might be connected to a particular phase of your life as a couple and, given space, can improve hugely.
- Discuss the use of porn, sex toys and other aids. A partner using (ethical) porn isn't a reflection on you – as long as it's not excessive. Used appropriately, it can add to your sex life, rather than detract from it.
- Talk about what you would like to do physically/sexually, what you feel like doing and – more especially – what you don't want to do.
- Take good care of your physical self: Pampering yourself through touch helps to connect your mind with your body (and genitals).

- Explore a compromise or agreed plan to work on it.
- Be compassionate with yourself and keep getting to know who you are as a person – a strong sense of self helps you to be appropriately vulnerable in your relationship.
- End any discussion on a positive note – not necessarily about sex, but your relationship.

If you've been abused...

Sexual abuse is a vast topic and important influence on intimacy. If you've experienced abuse, you may need specialist help to work your way through it. Apart from providing a safe space to tell your story, a therapist can help you understand your memories and doubts, and your negative and out-of-control reactions to sex, so you can separate abusive from healthy sexual experiences, and draw safe sexual and emotional boundaries in your relationship(s). It's important to know that, post-abuse, you can learn to be comfortable in your body – with all its related sensations, emotions and memories – and go on to enjoy healthy, satisfying sexual relationships.

2. Emotional intimacy

Arguably, emotional intimacy is the hardest to achieve. Plenty of people have sex (and enjoy it), but they never fully let go emotionally. Early in life, they erect an emotional wall and commit to living behind it. Plenty of people get away with it, too, although it stops them from having all the richness of an intimate relationship.

Simply put, emotional intimacy is the capacity for vulnerability, to bring your whole self – for better and worse – to the relationship. Couples who are friends before they get together have an advantage here, because they've already let their guard down, they've already shown at least glimpses of their true selves.

Vulnerability used to be considered a weakness but – largely thanks to the work of American researcher and author Dr Brené Brown, among others – it's now seen as an essential part of building closeness and fully being who you are. I feel like crying in relief at that change in perception. Some of the saddest people are those who live inside an emotional prison. Sure, the world demands that we don't walk around emotionally naked all the time. We have to pick and choose where we are vulnerable (and who with). Learning to be vulnerable takes work and carries risk. But the fact we now know and accept it's a good thing is gold.

Everyone has emotional needs within a relationship; we differ but, apart from love itself, the needs to feel heard, valuable, attractive/sexy and aligned (on the same page) make almost everyone's list, whether they're aware of it or not.

3. Intellectual and creative intimacy

This sounds high-brow but it doesn't mean 'higher level' anything. It just refers to a meeting of the minds, intellectually or creatively. While not essential, it can be a powerful bond. You don't have to be working in the same jobs or field, but being 'on the same wavelength' intellectually or creatively can be stimulating and feel surprisingly intimate. It's also the reason so many relationships, and affairs, begin at work.

An older woman told me that all she wanted in a new partner was someone she could talk to. She was a science researcher and she loved talking about global scientific issues. 'Sex is fine but, really, it's all about the conversation for me. I want to go to dinner and be interested in what they're saying. It doesn't even have to be a good dinner. Do you think I'm being too fussy?' she asked. I didn't, not at all. Why shouldn't intimacy be found in lofty scientific conversation over dinner, even if it's at a drive-through?

4. Spiritual intimacy

British applied psychologist Dr Pippa Grange describes intimacy as a 'gateway to the soul'. And, in full flight, I'd say that's true. I love the idea of spiritual intimacy. But first I should say this out loud: I don't believe in soulmates. So, people who are thinking there is One True Person out there for them – and they'll meet when all the stars align and the Moon hovers over the 7th Sun – shouldn't choose me as their therapist. We could build sound, loving relationships with many people in the world. It pays not to think about that, especially on a bad day in your relationship – it's smarter just to do your best with the one you're with.

Yes, compatible religious beliefs and spiritual alignment can help build intimacy. Spiritual intimacy can also just mean feeling connected to, or being 'in sync' with, your partner. Not all day, every day – that would be weird and possibly quite unhealthy. Rather, feeling in sync in all the little ways – your in-jokes; nicknames; favourite songs, movies, places and memories – all the things that have added to your history. And all those moments when things between you feel coincidental or 'right and easy', such as when you have a fleeting thought that you're happy to be with this person, and you know they're happy to be with you. When it just feels right. Ahhhh.

Your intimate needs

Here's how to assess your intimate needs. As in the following example, draw two circles and fill in the pie charts. If you're in a relationship, fill out the pie chart according to how your intimacy currently looks with your partner. Then, alongside it, complete the chart according to what you'd like it to look like. If you're not in a relationship, you can use this to guide what's important to you.

INTIMATE NEEDS

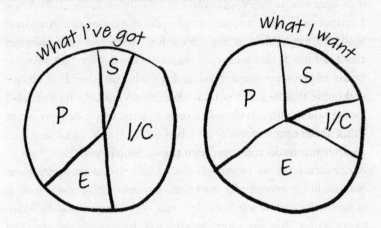

P: Physical (including sex)

E: Emotional

I/C: Intellectual / Creative

S: Spiritual (feeling in sync)

Analysing your needs

There's no 'ideal' state, as we're all different – the key is for what you've got to line up with what you want. If they do line up, your relationship is probably strong and stable.

If there's a discrepancy, think about how you could improve or grow the type of intimacy that's most important to you. Remember, there are other ways to have your intimate needs met; they don't all have to be met by your partner. In fact, expecting a partner to be 'everything' to you may put too much pressure on your relationship.

'Fear of intimacy' or emotional struggles?

Fear of intimacy is a commonly used psychological term, regarding worries about getting too close to someone. I don't use it – or even like it – because it turns these worries into the Great Wall of China, which makes everything seem too hard. Worries about intimacy don't need to be conquered; they just need to be acknowledged, understood and quietly put to bed. It always strikes me that 'fear' of intimacy is a tough evaluation of feelings that are quite normal when you've been hurt, either early in life or by a previous partner.

As we discussed in the Trust pillar, we all have issues about who to trust. As we should. It would be naïve to trust everyone, because not everyone gets into a relationship with good intent. It makes sense that if someone lets you down, you could be loath to try again. But the word fear evokes images of 'danger' and 'threat', which makes people who are wary of getting close to others feel like they're faulty. They're not – they're just acting on the experiences they've had and the messages they've received.

To reiterate, you can meet your intimate needs in ways other than through a partner. I first learned this from a police officer, who was perennially single (and loved it). She told me she got her intimacy at work. When I raised an eyebrow, she laughed. 'Not that,' she said, squashing the idea of affairs in the line of duty. She paused, grinning. 'Although maybe a couple of times.' She went on to explain. As a detective, her squad would go away on jobs, attend murder scenes, work late into the night, rely on each other for support, share hotel rooms, talk about everything from the case to their lives, and use black humour to cope with the trauma. 'It's such an intimate job in that way. I can't see how I could achieve that with a partner.'

Good point. Working closely together, and sharing traumatic or difficult experiences, like the police or military or in a hospital Emergency Department, can bond people tightly. Many relationships begin at work simply because spending a lot of time together promotes intimacy. But while work can be a way of fulfilling intimate needs, it can also be the wrong place to do it, or a shield to avoid getting close to someone in 'real life'.

Rather than 'fear' of intimacy, I prefer to think of it as an emotional struggle, in which a person finds it difficult to share their feelings and get close to another. People with these difficulties are often labelled 'emotionally unavailable', 'cold', 'evasive' or just hard to read. While this may be true (as in toxic relationships), it's a poor label. Some people have been bruised by loss and rejection, some are genuinely shy, others have just never had the benefit of an emotional education. For someone who genuinely struggles to let others in, love can be excruciating as well as frightening.

For a partner, however, this can be frustrating or confusing, particularly for those who 'wear their heart on their sleeve' emotionally or are a little insecure. It can cause the more open partner to harass the other about what's going on, which causes the closed one to back away.

If you struggle with the emotional side of intimacy (being fully available to a partner), or your partner does, some of these signs may resonate with you.

Key signs of emotional unavailability

1. They avoid the 'big' or 'deep' stuff.
Diving down into the world of emotion and feelings makes this person uncomfortable. They'll be happy to listen to their partner's emotional 'stuff' but only up to a point. When the subject matter gets too heavy, they'll change the subject. Talking about formal commitment may rattle them or even push them away.

2. They have intimacy in the same basket with something else.

An emotionally unavailable person often connects intimacy with high drama, conflict or inevitable loss/rejection – events from their past. This can make love feel confusing or frightening. It's easier to keep the guard up. For someone who, as a child or young person, carried heavy responsibility for a parent, intimacy may feel like a burden. This can mean that even when they are willing, they're not free to love for love's own sake. It feels uncomfortable or wrong.

3. They may struggle to ask for help.

When a person's been hurt or suffered significant loss, they struggle to enter relationships – even close friendships – with an open heart. That's because they're scared it'll happen again, and they can't bear the pain.

Even asking a partner for help can be difficult; they may find it easier to shut off.

4. They don't have an emotional 'language'.

The emotionally unavailable person can't put their feelings into words. It may be that they never learned to match words with their feelings, or had sound emotional expression modelled to them. It's not that they don't have feelings. They may have plenty; they just don't know how to release them appropriately.

5. They cut people out of their life easily, often without reason.

Relationships – including friendships and family ties – can be terminated suddenly and without explanation. Think ghosting, but it can also involve walking away from a long-term bond. It is hurtful, and confusing, if you're on the end of it. These acts may have a toxic agenda. But also, an emotionally unavailable person can think it's easier to kill off a relationship than wade through an explanation of why.

6. They're most comfortable with people outside their day-to-day orbit.

They will often choose relationships they can keep at arm's length. Affairs, long-distance relationships, people who aren't free to commit to them. It's less stressful to keep some space, with no pressure to move the relationship forward. They may even choose friendships that don't make emotional demands on them.

7. They respond to others' feelings rather than offering their own.

They'll often find it easy to show a lot of interest in you, especially at the beginning of a relationship, because asking questions is non-threatening. It can be seductive because it makes you feel fascinating, but it also keeps you away from their feelings, which is the whole point.

What does it mean?

People who have emotional intimacy difficulties aren't necessarily toxic or make 'bad' partners. There may be genuine reasons for emotional difficulties, such as shyness and insecurity, or having a difficult history. With patience, and where trust is carefully and patiently built, they can make excellent mates.

If you struggle with this and you'd like things to change, remember that trust is attained by slow degrees. There's no rush, as long as you're both willing. It may also be worth considering professional help, because it can make a huge difference to what you bring to relationships and what you get from them.

If your partner has these issues, you need to consider your experience of being with them. It's great (and important) to be patient and supportive, but a relationship shouldn't be persistently hard and confusing. If you're doing all the heavy lifting and/or it makes you feel anxious or bad about yourself, you need to ask if being with them is worth it. Your life – and happiness – matters too.

Loneliness: Playing on your own

Many people on their own report cravings for intimacy. Emotionally yes, but also just for physical touch. People's experiences during the COVID-19 pandemic have brought a fresh empathy for those who don't have the opportunity to connect with others, who never get a hug.

Being on your own can be tough if it's not what you signed on for, or ever wanted. Even if you want to be on your own, it can have its challenges. I recall a confident 40-year-old single man who utterly rejected the life he saw his friends, who had young children, having. 'It just looks like a lot of nagging and conflict, and very little affection to me.' But he conceded there was a warmth to their lives that he was missing. 'I loved being on my own at 30, but I'm not so sure anymore,' he finally said. A year later, he met a woman and his childhood trauma floated to the surface. His confidence vanished; he was like a teenager on a first date. He had wanted love all along, but his high standards were a cover for his fear.

There's another loneliness related to relationships that many are uncomfortable talking about – the loneliness of losing your intimate connection with your partner. As one woman said, 'How can I complain to my single friend about feeling lonely when I'm married? I'm not alone in the house. Surely, I have it better than she does?'

Loneliness within relationships is possibly more common than is thought; studies suggest that up to 40 per cent of people in partnerships feel lonely. This is more than a communication drift, it's isolation – even a coldness – within a relationship.

People often report feeling shut out when their partner is going through a tough time, but they can't (or won't) share their feelings. Or their partner can't, or is unwilling to, be there for them emotionally. If that sounds like you, use these questions to tap into what's going on and find a way forward.

1. What's changed?

Assuming you once felt close and loving towards your partner, what has changed? And how long has it been this way? It's helpful if you can pin down the reason – and, if possible, a timeframe. That gives you a base from which to start talking about it, and making a change or two. Even one small tweak, or adding something new to the mix, can make you feel more hopeful.

2. Has trauma/stress sabotaged you?

Stress can come at us from all directions. With everyone working and chores piling up, families are under time and financial pressure just to survive – let alone thrive. Stress can affect everything, from mood and emotional reactions to the home/family environment, to your libido. Check in on your stress levels and those of your partner and, if they're off the charts, get together and brainstorm ways you can bring them down.

3. Is there someone else?

The appearance of 'someone else' frequently sparks feelings of loneliness within relationships. It may not be a full-blown affair or even inappropriate messaging – it may just be someone who listens to you, or you have fun with. But it highlights the gap between *what you have now* and *what you could have*. This song can play overtime in your head, driving you crazy with thoughts of *What if* … So analyse what's going on inside your relationship before you opt to play outside it.

4. Is your partner lonely, too?

Consumed by negative feelings, we tend to overlook what might be going on for someone else. It may be that you and your partner are sitting side-by-side on the sofa every evening, with the same feelings: *I'd rather be somewhere else.* Don't bottle those feelings: ask your partner how they're feeling. You might not get the answer you want but, either way, it's information you need to know.

5. Is loneliness a pattern for you?
If you've been lonely in a previous relationship, you'll feel it even more intensely the second (or third) time. If it's a pattern, it's worth taking a look at your inter-relational style. Perhaps you've been looking to your partner to fill a void for you and they're no longer doing it? Consider what you expect and need from a partner; perhaps get an outside view as to whether it's realistic, and what you could do to fill that void yourself.

6. Is social media playing with you?
Social media can alleviate loneliness by allowing you to stay connected to others without much pressure. It can also twist the knife on you by forcing a comparison between your tired relationship and the happy, glowing pictures of other couples online. Remember, no couples post pictures of themselves on a bad day. So ask yourself, is your social media use making you feel better, neutral or worse about your relationship? Then act accordingly.

7. Has life got boring?
Maybe your life has become predictable; maybe you're just bored. And that's made you focus on your relationship as the component that needs resuscitation. Be careful not to load your partner with responsibility for your choices and happiness. Be honest about what's going on for you and what you could do to spark your life, interest and curiosity. Most of all, be sure to step back and look at your life broadly. Your relationship is part of your life – not the whole deal.

Barriers to intimacy

What might block our attempts or ability to be intimate is a question that therapists often examine. Many present as sexual difficulties – or that's what couples say – but sexual problems are often symptomatic of deeper issues, such as the messages they received about sex as a young person (e.g. that sex is wrong, dirty, bad or should be saved for marriage).

Not always, though. Many couples still have sex – even if it's not as good as it once was – when they are emotionally drifting apart. It's the emotional separation that often causes the most pain.

Many factors can block or limit intimacy. Beyond historical beliefs and the early messages we picked up around sex and trust, intimacy can be affected by stress and fatigue, conflict, addictions, mental health issues, infidelity, body-image problems, and self-criticism. Sometimes, just repetition and lack of fun can eat away at previously solid relationships.

We need to talk (more) about sex

Even though sex is just one part of intimacy, it's what grabs centre stage. It's easier to identify sex as a problem in a relationship because people 'get' sex. That is, they know if they're having it or not; they know if it's good, bad, boring or painful; and they know if they want lots of it, they don't want it or they no longer want it. They know if their partner wants more or less sex than they do. They can tell you they schedule it for Tuesday night when the kids are at soccer practice. They can (hopefully) tell you what they like in bed and what their partner likes, and doesn't like. They can tell you they feel resentful about not getting enough sex, or guilty about not wanting or having more. The point is, gathering data on your sex life is relatively easy – or at least, it's easier than working out the degree of drift in your emotional connection.

What people don't know about sex is how much other people are having. They think everyone else is having a lot more fun than they are, and it drives them crazy. Perhaps it's the privilege of therapy that allows me to say this – because people are honest when their partners can't hear them – but everyone is having a lot less sex than they admit they are. Certainly, they're having a lot less good sex.

Even though we are enlightened people, living in an enlightened age, there's a part of us that believes other people are having sex as they do in Hollywood: hot and heavy, in darkened doorways, on deserted beaches or on kitchen benches, at any age and stage. The truth is that, a few years into married life, the last thing you want is sex on the bench where you cut the school lunches. Bodies, sexual arousal, desire, orgasm and needs change. Desire doesn't leap eagerly into bed with habit and repetition. And if everyone understood, accepted and talked about it, it would save so much angst.

Intimacy in relationships is about more than sex – lots more. If you base all your intimate needs on sex, you will struggle. But when you combine sex, or physical intimacy, with other kinds of closeness, you have a chance of going the distance – happily.

We need to talk about porn, too

Porn is a key influence on intimacy, not just through sex itself, but its impact on emotional connection. A billion-dollar growth industry, porn is a huge challenge for modern relationships, especially for those who've grown up alongside it. Just as sex is a subset of intimacy, porn is a subset of sex. Or the kind of sex it takes to create a loving, healthy relationship.

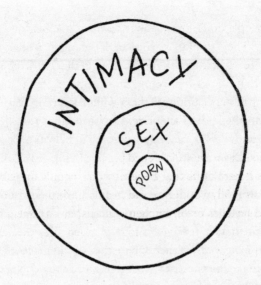

Watching ethically produced porn (and using it to masturbate) can be a healthy, harm-free part of a person's sex life, whether they're in a relationship or single. Used appropriately, it can help couples who have different sex drives or struggle with sex for various reasons.

In relationships, however, partners may have differing views about porn, about what's appropriate and how it should be used. This can cause tension. Studies indicate that porn use is linked to less satisfaction in relationships, but researchers concede this may be due to the lack of other skills, such as managing conflict or emotional regulation.

When porn is used inappropriately, it can threaten a person's mental health, social development and capacity for intimacy. Most therapists have seen people who've had difficulties with porn – both those with addictions and the partners of heavy porn-users – who struggle with trust, intimate relationships and their own self-worth. Another problem that's often mentioned is the time porn takes up; while their partner stays up to 'meet their needs' online, they will go to bed alone.

When is porn a problem?

Heavy or addictive porn use can lead to the following
problems:

- Setting expectations that sex will be a certain way, and
  that people must sculpt or shave themselves to look
  certain ways if they want someone to be with – or even
  like – them.
- Teaching that sexual gratification is a quick thing; you
  don't need to take time with talking, manners, emotional
  connection, and listening to your partner's needs and
  desires.
- Implying that violence and certain sexual practices are
  common and acceptable, and that you should expect your
  partner to go along with them.
- Ignoring the need to control sexual urges, which can
  both hurt people and cross legal boundaries.
- Believing that sex with a partner is your right, and that
  everyone wants it as much, and as often, as you do.
- Dismissing or undervaluing all that goes with a loving
  relationship, apart from sex.
- Needing porn to achieve orgasm and being unable to
  function healthily with a partner.

If you're a porn user, or it's a feature of your relationship,
you need to ask if it's having a negative impact, sexually
or emotionally. Check that it is (1) not taking up excessive
amounts of time; (2) not impacting other areas of life such
as study, healthy, work, sleep and other activities; and (c) not
hurting significant others. If you get a green light in all
three areas, then porn is probably not going to harm your
relationship – unless the type and frequency of use changes.

Hot, then not: Changes in sexual intimacy

A client asked me, 'How do you prevent boredom in a relationship?'

'Do you mean sexually?' I asked, innocently. I knew he did.

'All sorts of boredom,' he said, then laughed. 'Okay, yes, I mean sex. I mean, I just don't see how it's possible to stay interested in the same person, year after year. It's surely gonna get old.'

At the time, he was a year into a relationship and enjoying it very much. But his history was telling him that he would become bored in time, like he saw in his mates and their relationships. After a bit, he conceded that he would probably bore his partner, too.

I smiled. He was an astute man, with a genuine desire to have a lasting relationship and a family. But, at 28, he also understood his own sexual drive and need. In his teens and early 20s, he'd been completely driven by sex. 'How do people do it?' he asked. 'How do they keep it interesting, year after year?'

Good point. There are so many factors involved in sexual interest or loss of it: lust, hormones, pheromones, love, tenderness, devotion and stress relief … or guilt. I could go on. There are so many things that erode it: stress, illness, surgery, childbirth, body changes, hormones, menopause, lack of sleep, parenting, life circumstances and the simple fact that we all grow older.

It would have been deceitful to say that, even when both he and his partner were fully engaged in the relationship, their sexual desire would remain dialled up and perfectly matched. Perhaps it's possible but, if so, it's rare. While there are ways of keeping sex interesting through the years, it's healthier and more realistic to look at intimacy broadly, rather than pinning it all on sex. Sexual satisfaction may lie not in meeting someone new, but in learning to look at your partner differently.

My client agreed it was a good idea to keep working on their connection, rather than just their sex life. Here are some more ideas to help.

- **Be physically comfortable when you're talking.** It doesn't have to mean being curled up on the couch. You can be out for a walk or drive, or sharing a leisure activity. Don't make it too intense. It can be easier to chat while 'doing' rather than holding eye contact.

- **Touch.** Physical contact of any kind creates feelings of intimacy. Physical touch without the pressure of it always leading to sex is important, and your partner will appreciate it.

- **Lighten up.** This doesn't mean joking around about serious problems or issues, or always keeping things on the surface. But try not to be too heavy about everything. It's okay to smile and laugh (appropriately) even when discussing deep issues. Keeping a deadpan, serious face doesn't improve relationship outcomes.

- **Don't judge or criticise.** It sounds obvious, but we can all do with a reminder. Criticism creates distance and, when constant, will open a yawning gap.

- **Hang on to your (good) history.** When a relationship is going through a tough time, it's important to hang on to the reasons you got into it and your happy memories – favourite song/music, movies, holidays. And appreciate your couple rituals, all those little things you do for each other: they enhance relationships. Remind yourself of them often.

- **Do something your partner enjoys.** Even if it's not your favourite thing, even if you've got your own 'stuff' to do, spend time doing their activities. Not grudgingly, though, with a smile on your face.

- **Be complimentary.** Physically and in other ways, too. Especially if you see your partner has made an effort to dress up or look nice, or with something that is really important to them. If they're self-critical, you'll be helping to counter it.

- **Say what you like, sexually or otherwise.** A lot of people sit on the fence in their relationship, hoping to keep the peace or let their partner decide. This can be stressful for a loving partner, because they don't know what you're really feeling. You don't have to thump the table with your demands (I'm not advocating for that), but speak up for what you like and want to do. There's an exercise coming up to help in terms of your sexual preferences.
- **Talk about future plans.** The vision of a shared future will draw you closer – as long as you both want, and buy into, the same things.

Sex-positive environments: Your ideal 'conditions'

When you first get together with someone, you may be up for having sex any time, anywhere. The conditions don't matter; it can be that the more outrageous the circumstances, the better. But few couples maintain this over time. It's helpful to revisit what works for you (and what absolutely doesn't). Talk with your partner about it, so they know how to create it and also when not to push it.

Creating a sex-positive environment helps arousal because, in the simplest terms, humans have a brain-to-genital connection – especially women. Women's sexual response is more sensitive to context; that is, both the surroundings and their mental state.

Reflect on your ideal conditions for sex. People are often shy about sharing their sexual desires and preferences with their partner, but silence will never make it better. You don't need to make it a huge in-depth exercise. Just start with some simple prompt questions to figure out what works best for you.

My ideal time of day/week for sex is

....

What kind of sexual interaction do I like/respond to best?

....

What's the right physical environment to get me in the mood? (e.g. bedroom, lighting, smell)

....

What makes me feel desired?

....

How do I feel about my health/body during sex?

....

What is the effect of life stress on my ability to engage in sex?

....

Do I like to initiate or be pursued?

....

What do I enjoy about sex?

....

Can I achieve sexual relief without a partner?

....

When do I absolutely not want to (or can't) engage in sex?

....

What sexual activities make me uncomfortable/
I don't want to do?

....

What could my partner do to themselves make me feel more positive about sex?

....

What could my partner do for me to make me feel more positive about sex?

....

My idea of satisfying sex is

....

Intimacy exercise: How well do you know that person in your bed?

You wake up next to someone. You make coffee. You eat toast. You wade through the morning chaos. You go to work. You come home. You get through the evening chaos. You pour wine. You stream a TV show. You go to bed.

You look across the sheets. There's your partner scrolling their phone; you've been with them for years, the one you know so well. But do you? Do you really know the one you're with?

Here's a quiz to test just that.

Testing intimacy

Note: Part A is easy. Part B is a little more demanding and Part C takes you to the heart of the big stuff.

Warning: It's fine to ask these questions of yourself, but be careful about confronting your partner with them. Their answers might surprise (or scare) you.

Part A: Easy terrain

- What first attracted you to your partner?
- Where/what was your first (official) date?
- What was your partner's favourite kind of date back then? What is it now?
- What's your partner's favourite thing to do when not working?
- What three words would you use to describe your partner?

Part B: Intermediate grade

- What three words would your partner use to describe you?
- How does your partner react to stress? (What do they feel/do?)

- How long do they stay locked in that reaction? What helps them break out of it?
- What upsets your partner?
- What makes your partner most happy?
- Who is most important to your partner (besides you and family)?

Part C: Difficult (tread with care)

- What was your partner's childhood dream?
- If your partner could make a wish come true now, what would it be?
- What is your partner's biggest regret?
- What's your partner's biggest worry? What could be done to alleviate it?
- Is your partner happy? With you? Generally? (Why or why not?)

What does it all mean?

Were you surprised with what you knew, or didn't know? A little worried? Or did you come in top of the class?

Most people fly through Part A, are more thoughtful with B, and struggle with C – especially the question about regret. Try it if you're brave enough. There are often big ghosts in the cupboard, even when couples have been together a long time.

The question relating to your partner's happiness can be challenging, but it doesn't help to hide from it. There can be all sorts of reasons for someone's discontent in a relationship and, if your partner is unhappy, you don't have to take full responsibility for it or fix it. Your first step is just to open the door for them to talk about it.

People often say they crave more depth in their relationships. But every conversation you have with your partner doesn't have to be deep and meaningful. Boring if it was! I'm always surprised when people want to dive deep with their partners all the time. The idea of it makes me feel exhausted. Half the fun of a relationship is the light stuff – the banter, the easy laughs that come with knowing someone for a long time. (As long as your relationship isn't just all banter, causing you to ignore important topics.)

***

We spend a lot of time thinking about ourselves, and our own hopes and dreams. That's important – but not at the expense of the hopes and dreams of your partner.

So try this. Next time you're alone with your partner, ask them something more interesting than you might usually. There's no need to bolt into the abyss with the huge questions. But try to go beyond the house, the kids, the neighbours, your jobs and the local gossip. Ask something that makes them think; even when the answer is not what you were expecting, it may be helpful to your relationship to hear it.

Finally, consider this: *What would make the biggest (positive) difference to your partner's life right now?* Then see if you can help make it happen.

Still on the subject of knowing your partner, here's another fun measure you can use to test your knowledge of them.

***

The ultimate relationship challenge

This has been adapted from the BBC podcast series *Desert Island Discs*. Your partner is a castaway on a desert island. You must answer the following questions to get them back (assuming you want them back!). When you're done, check to see if you got the answers right. Then switch it up and see if they can pick your answers.

- How would your partner react to the isolation of the island? (And the sudden change in circumstances?)
- How would they occupy their time?
- What would they eat/drink (given a choice)?
- They can have one video call. Who would it be (apart from you)?
- What music/reading material would they insist on taking?
- What luxury item would they choose to take?
- What could they not live without

Obviously, there is no pass or fail grade. It's just another way of testing your knowledge of your partner and, perhaps more usefully, yourself.

Intimacy: Quick takeaways

- Secrets are a (huge) barrier to intimacy.
- Few people are having as much sex as you think they are.
- No-one is having as much GOOD sex as you think they are.
- There are different kinds of intimacy – if you rely solely on sex, you'll run into trouble.
- There are many paths to feeling emotionally connected.
- Worries about intimacy don't need to be conquered – just understood.
- *What would make the biggest difference to your partner's life right now?* This is a great question.
- It's a great question to ask about your own life, too.

PILLAR 5:
LOAD-SHARING

Do you give and take equally?

'Housework won't kill you, but then again, why take the chance?'

– Phyllis Diller

Why does it matter? Load-sharing between partners involves the domestic chores and the household's emotional load, obviously, but also thoughts and feelings, hurts and worries, and hopes and dreams. Sharing is closely connected to trust. It's also the opposite of laziness, which will undermine even healthy relationships.

***

Do you carry your share of the domestic load? By that, I don't just mean the housework (studies show this causes friction between 80 per cent of people who live with a partner), but the emotional labour – all the 'invisible stuff' that couples, families and people in shared living arrangements need to run efficiently, or even at all.

While both types of domestic load can lead to fatigue, conflict and resentment, it's the emotional, or cognitive, labour that often gets people down, because it's the hardest to identify or share.

Emotional labour includes all the family 'intel', such as which child has allergies, and who likes what in their lunch box, which kid needs new football boots or a plate to take to their class shared lunch, and who has a playdate on Saturday. It's also who's remembering to call the electrician, pick up the dry-cleaning and get the dog in for grooming. It may also include being the household disciplinarian, which can divide couples into 'good' and 'bad' cop roles.

Many couples aim for a 50:50 split of domestic responsibilities. However, studies show that, in heterosexual relationships, women still do the bulk of the housework and childcare. A growing body of research shows that even when such couples achieve an equal split, women carry significantly more of the emotional or 'hidden' load than men. In single-parent families, the bigger burden falls on women, who are up to 80 per cent more likely than men to be a primary caregiver.

It is also far more common for women, struggling with all the demands on them, to raise the divide in therapy. One woman said:

'I can get my husband to vacuum and he's a pretty good cook, but he just doesn't remember all that other stuff – his brain doesn't work like that. He tells me to write him a list and he'll do everything on it. He will, too. He's always keen to help – but just the act of writing that list means I never get away from the weight of it. If I went away, the place would collapse. Don't think I haven't considered it, just so they can find out how much I do!'

If this resonates, you're absolutely not alone. While most studies do point to gender differences, it's important to remember there can be other individual issues at the heart of these conflicts. To illustrate, here's Pip's story.

When the laundry never ends: Pip's story

Pip feels like she's sinking in a quicksand of laundry.

'I know that's dramatic,' she says, but laundry is the one thing that never goes away. Sorting, washing, drying, folding, putting away ... then around we go again. I'm exhausted.'

Pip is a primary school teacher. She and her partner, Talia, have two daughters, aged six and three. Talia also has a 13-year-old son, Zac, from a previous relationship. Talia works in sales, which means she is often away midweek for work.

It's a 'crazy, busy' household, Pip says. She works a full day at school, then races to pick up the girls, gets dinner on, organises the household, and tries to supervise homework and keep everyone off their devices. Zac has sports training and other activities in the evenings, but they all try to have dinner together.

After dinner comes the dishes, sorting school/daycare lunches and random odd jobs. Pip then turns to her teaching paperwork and planning for the next day. She barely watches television but has a 'thing' for social media – it's how she catches up with friends. 'I'm often folding laundry at midnight.'

Weekends are no better. It's a mad rush between chores, life admin, stocking up at the supermarket, the kids' activities and trying to do at least one 'fun family thing' before the new week begins. She also takes meals to her mother, who recently broke her ankle and lives a half-hour drive away.

Talia spends a lot of time with her family, including caring for her elderly parents. This causes friction.

'Tal helps out when she can, but she's often not here and she's much more relaxed about the state of the house than I am,' Pip says. 'She's the fun parent and I'm the tough one, which I resent. She says I need to chill out. Half the time, she just doesn't see what needs to be done and she doesn't remember all the little stuff, such as buying a birthday present for someone's party, or what we've run out of in the pantry. It drives me crazy.'

Pip admits she's a little obsessive about cleaning. 'But there's just so much to do. I never seem to get clear of it. Tal and I fight about it, but we never really sort it out.'

We talk for a while about some ways she could better manage, or share, the load. When we discuss how she could better divide the chores, steal some 'me time', ask Talia for help or organise Zac to do more, she pushes back. There's a BUT to every one of my suggestions.

Eventually, she looks at me quizzically. 'I'm coming up with excuses for all your ideas.'

I smile. 'So you noticed, then. Why do you think you're doing that when you're so exhausted? Could there be a reason you don't want things to change?'

She sits quietly for a while. 'It's what I do and I'm good at it. I need to be valued. I'm the rock of this family and I like it that way.'

Deep in the chore wars

Pip and Talia's lives are frantic, but they're no different from many other families, who have their foot on the pedal trying to run their domestic households, maintain their careers, bring in money, and care for kids and elderly parents.

Most need both partners to work fulltime to pay their mortgage and sustain their lifestyles. This puts everyone under stress, which can lead to niggles and conflict within a relationship, as well as quietly eating away at mental wellbeing. Pip constantly feels guilty she's not doing enough. She's already exhibiting signs of psychological stress: poor sleeping, irritability, weight gain, headaches, lack of focus (she calls it 'brain fog'), finding no fun in anything – and, without change, she may find herself tipping into the depression-anxiety zone.

Pip has historical reasons for why she struggles to ask for

help but, even with help, she'd be staggering under the load. In the busyness of 21st-century life, there's just a lot to do. While some people take on more than they should and STILL feel guilty, others are avoidant – some because they just don't see what needs to be done, others because they're lazy – and the clash can breed problems.

Kids: The hidden emotional load

There's one more type of emotional labour: Kids. True, kids also fall into both other categories – they require a lot of physical time and energy, and anticipating and meeting all their needs sucks up a fair amount of mental energy.

What you're not prepared for, however, is a different kind of emotional load – the worry that goes with them. The sheer and huge *responsibility* that comes with being a parent to someone who needs you so much. And it never, ever stops.

When my kids were little, I developed a fear of flying. I'm not anxious and I'd never worried about flying previously, but my new fear came in the same package as my new responsibility. Fear of flying never became a full-blown phobia, but I white-knuckled the armrests when I felt the sudden burden of how essential I was to my kids, that they couldn't live without me. My free-spirited days were over, I couldn't take risks anymore – and I wasn't sure I liked it.

While my fear of flying went away, I still worry about my kids, even though they are young women now. I worry when they break up with their partners, get fired, are unemployed, get hurt, get sick, have setbacks or disappointments, and all the little mothery bits in between. All this takes up space in my mind, space that I'm going to need more than ever as my executive brain function slows down with age.

Some researchers file parental worry under 'emotional labour', but I think it needs a category of its own. While it's generally considered a more female issue (statistics show women worry more than men about everything), I wouldn't want to claim that for sure. Plenty of men worry about their kids, and some mothers don't at all. But I do know my husband – who loves our daughters equally – has always been better able to detach. Especially on the golf course.

We all know this worry is what you get when you sign on for parenting – and research will never be able to measure that kind of love. But it's still important to acknowledge parental worry as hugely emotionally taxing, because it is. And it can be an extremely difficult load to divide and share equally.

Micromanagement and perfectionism: Loaded issues

Academics say issues around housework are less about the housework and more about other needs, such as feeling heard, understood and valued. That is often true – as in Pip's case – and it can be helpful to explore these issues. But even when there are psychological reasons underpinning 'chore behaviour', it's unfair to attribute the conflict to one partner's issues. In any household, there's a heap to do, so a compromise must be found.

One of the key problems with chores is that couples have different expectations about how, when, and how well, things should be done. This can lead to one partner feeling like they're having to give too much direction (also known as 'nagging') while the other feels like they're being micromanaged (also known as 'being nagged'). Or perhaps one partner has such high – or even perfectionist – standards that the other can never reach them, which can cause conflict on both sides.

Micromanagement and perfectionism often go hand in hand. Here's an explanation of both and strategies to help minimise conflict.

Micromanagement at home

'My boss is a micromanager!' You've almost certainly heard that term in a workplace setting. Micromanaging is a style in which the boss hangs over your shoulder, watching, controlling, critiquing and making (often unwanted or needed) 'suggestions'. At best, it's annoying; at worst, it's bullying.

It can be stressful in the workplace, especially if you spend 40 hours a week there, but at least you can get away from it. When it happens at home, however, micromanaging can be a source of bubbling conflict.

Domestic micromanagement is softer than the office version; it's not bullying, it often just comes down to one person needing to take chief responsibility for domestic life. But it can also be a form of anxiety. When the micromanaging partner is *across everything* that's going on domestically, they feel better – and calmer.

Domestic micromanagers often have extremely high standards, so they don't trust their partners to do things as well as they do. (It may also be that they feel they have to do everything because their partner doesn't step up.)

A danger with micromanagement is that it leads to frustration all round, with one partner resentful because they're carrying the full burden, and the other increasingly indecisive and feeling useless.

Here are some signs there's some micromanaging going on in your relationship. Remember, none of these signs stands in isolation – being busy, for example, is just the nature of life. Use this list to consider your role in the relationship.

Tick those that apply to you:

❑ You're always busy, you never seem to have any free time.
❑ You struggle to delegate.
❑ You run an extremely tidy and organised household.
❑ You organise the social calendar, and your partner mostly comes along for the ride.

❏ You're a big planner – you like to know 'what's happening'.

❏ As a couple, you mostly do what you like/want to do.

❏ You're a details person and/or a big list maker.

❏ You are way more across what's going on in the household than your partner.

❏ You're decisive on the home front.

❏ You feel guilty when you're relaxing or taking 'me time'.

❏ Your partner often says they can't meet your standards.

❏ You feel like you don't get enough help at home.

❏ You do most domestic 'things' better than your partner.

Lots of ticks? Maybe you've identified a tendency to micromanage? If you have few ticks, then maybe you've seen these tendencies in your partner?

That's okay, an imbalance in how we run our domestic households often happens slowly, or when kids come into the mix. So it's not the fault of one or the other – you're both responsible for how your shared life operates.

If you're BOTH happy with the arrangement, all good. You only need to consider change if it's causing angst on either side.

Perfectionism at home

My client Josh confessed he was a clean and tidiness freak. He was up cleaning up after dinner before his partner had finished eating. If she cleaned the bathroom, he would do it again after her, just to bring it up to standard.

Josh was well aware of the impact this had on his partner – how it made her feel inadequate and that she'd wasted her time, and how it could cause her to stop trying to contribute altogether. But he struggled to put the brakes on himself.

'I'm really, really trying,' he said. 'But I'm a better cleaner than she is. I can't function properly without order. A messy or unclean house stresses me out. And I want us both to come home to a nice environment.'

I chose this example because, like most therapists, I generally hear it the other way round – from women. While I don't want to undermine the fact that women generally carry the greater domestic burden, it's worth noting men can struggle in this area, too.

Needing order or cleanliness to feel calm often goes unreported, but it's valid. Many studies have connected tidy or clean spaces with improved mental wellbeing. It's no wonder that 'organisation porn' is now a thing; many people are making a lot of money out of our need for control in at least one aspect of our lives.

There's no denying the benefits, either. Any form of exercise (even cleaning) is good for us, because it moves the body and releases endorphins. Cleaning can also help you park your worries and 'be present' (as in mindfulness) when you are fully engaged in a cleaning task.

People struggling with stress or mental health issues often report feeling better when they've decluttered or cleaned their personal space.

Josh, like many, was a 'stress cleaner'. He used it to ease his anxiety. It took his mind away from his worries, and a feeling of order helped him to chill out. It's fine to clean for these reasons, as long as it doesn't turn into a compulsion (excessive behaviour driven by obsessive, irrational thoughts) or is used to make the other person feel bad, both of which can put the relationship at risk.

Even if you don't struggle with micromanagement or perfectionism, it's worth checking in on what's going on at home, so you can head off difficulties before they tip into resentment.

Here are some things to think about and some strategies.

Own your role (and your WHY).

Ask yourself hard questions: *Are you happy with the arrangement you've settled into? Are you proud of your role? Are you who you want to be in the relationship?*

Is it contributing to your health and happiness? If you are happy – and your partner is too – then nothing needs to change.

But if you're not … be honest about your chores. *Are you doing too much? Are you exhausted because of them? Are your standards too high? Do you struggle to delegate because you know you'll do things better than everyone else?*

Don't put a label on yourself. Just because you're the domestic 'leader' doesn't mean you are controlling or micromanaging, or a perfectionist. It may be that, like Pip and Josh, you're doing it for other reasons. It may be because of your temperament or your need to feel calm and in control. There's no shame in that. But just be honest with yourself about your WHY.

Who's lying on the couch?

Once you've been honest with yourself about what you do, it's easier to take a look at your partner's input, and that of anyone else who shares your home.

Check your partner's input. Is the load-share fair? Are you coping with all you have to do? How could you divide up the chores better? If your partner is a perennial couch-dweller, it's definitely not fair. Have an honest chat with them (not when either of you is angry!) about the split of responsibility and tasks – and about how you feel about them. Listen to what they have to say.

It may be that they leave it all to you because you do it best. Or they feel inadequate. Or they don't know what to do. These things can all be worked on.

Divide but don't rule.

Figure out a fair split. Ask your partner which chores they'd like to be responsible for. Play to your strengths – a person who likes to cook, or is good at it, is far more likely to take charge of the evening meal than someone who finds it challenging. Just because your best friend's partner is a superb cook, doesn't mean your partner should turn into one.

P.S. There's no such thing as being good at nothing. Everyone has a strength, or they need to cultivate one. Quickly.

Create a practical (reasonable) routine together.

Everyone functions better with routine. Everyone functions better when they know their contribution makes THEIR life better, too. Just saying.

The key is to involve everyone, including the kids, in creating the routine. If you just hand out a list of chores, you'll get push-back – guaranteed. If you work it out together and everyone agrees at the outset, it's much harder for them to renege on their responsibilities.

There's no such thing as 'Over-Thanking'.

Say thank you, liberally. I recall one client who'd become quite embittered by her partner's laziness. She felt resentful at the thought of thanking him for doing things *he should have done anyway*. He didn't thank her, so *why should she thank him*? It was probably fair enough but, psychologically, it was a bad strategy. It's a natural human drive to want to feel appreciated and valued. The more people feel they are valued (and loved), the more they will contribute, as long as they are a vaguely decent person. I always say to my clients there's no such thing as Over-Thanking. If it's genuine (and delivered without sarcasm), it's an easy way to get big results. Or at least some more help.

Keep the higher goal in mind.

When we get into conflicts, it's easy to lose sight of why we're in a relationship – or why we ever thought it was a good idea. Which is a bad way to operate, because it makes us say and do things that are too harsh and mean, and which we later regret.

When you go into a meeting at work, you have (or should have) the outcome in mind. That is, what you want, or hope, to achieve. It's exactly the same in a relationship. If you approach the 'chore wars' wanting things to be better, because you love this person and you want to be with them, you'll get much better outcomes.

If you let the resentment simmer and rise until you explode, then explode again … well, even if you have the best of reasons, you may be taking your relationship down a darker road than you should, especially if – underneath it all – you love your partner.

'Me Time': Putting yourself first

When it comes to domestic sharing, the chore wars are only one trap. Enter 'Me Time'. We all know that 'me time' is important, that it's healthy to carve out time for ourselves to do our own thing, even if it's just to slow the heart rate between the never-ending demands of work, home and life admin.

But what about when you have to barricade yourself in the bathroom just to get a few minutes to yourself, as a toddler screams at the door or a teenager grunts in the lounge?

What about when your partner heads for the gym, then out for a drink after, while you stay home fighting the avalanche of 'stuff' you have to do?

What is it about their cheerful goodbye that makes you burn with resentment?

***

The battle between couples for 'me time' often slips into a point-scoring exercise between couples: if you do that, then I can do this. If you go out Friday, then I'm going out Saturday. If you go on that winery/brewery crawl, then I'm going on a camping trip. Me this, you that. While it's an obvious way for both partners to get their own needs met, it can become a contest, especially when one is seen to be getting more freedom than the other. It becomes a grab for time, rather than a gracious giving of needed space.

While women more often report a lack of 'me time', increasing numbers of men – especially younger men, who are conscious of making an equal contribution at home – also struggle with this. I've seen both men and women work a full day, rush to pick up kids – and groceries – then help out with the 'witching hours', before returning to their laptops to put in another few hours before bed. Everyone's exhausted, everyone's guilty that they're not doing more (either working or helping out at home or spending time with their partner or family), and everyone's frustrated that they don't get more free time. And many, particularly women, feel a double dose of guilt when they grab even a little time for themselves.

Nearly everyone who talks about their relationships in therapy mentions 'me time' – mainly their frustration in not getting any. Even if they don't raise it, I do. When we don't get time to unwind, we raise the risk of burnout – emotionally, physically and in our relationships. Having time to yourself can make a huge difference to your health and wellbeing. But not having any can make you lose your way as an individual – you can forget who you truly are and what you like to do. And that can breed resentment.

Playing snatch 'n' grab for time is a fact of life for almost every couple, especially when you have kids. Even former US First Lady Michelle Obama who, dare I say, had more access to domestic help than most, struggled with this. In one interview, she spoke about women's struggle to put themselves first and the conflict that brews when one partner gets more time to themselves than the other. She talked of how husband Barack always managed to prioritise himself. When they had babies, he still went to the gym – every day. Michelle battled to find the time, and make the effort, to look after herself. 'I was like, how do you find time to work out? Let me stop being mad at him for going to the gym and let me get to the gym.' This was one of the issues that prompted them to get counselling, she said.

That's validating for us all. Finding 'me time' can be challenging and feel selfish but, ultimately, taking time for your own health and needs benefits your relationship and family.

How to know when you need more 'me time'

It's worth keeping an eye on how you're feeling because having no time – and giving relentlessly to others – can erode your mental health. It's slower, but it's still a hazard.

Here are signs you're heading down that path:

- You can't name when you last had fun.
- You constantly feel irritable with people you love.
- You can barely face taking a phone call – even from a good friend.
- You always feel overwhelmed and ineffective.
- You've become more negative and cynical about people and life generally.
- You've lost motivation to stick to healthy habits (e.g. eating well, drinking in moderation, regular exercise).
- Even when you get 'me time', you can't get fired up about using it. Or you're not sure what to do with it.

Creating more time for ME

'Me time' is simply time free from obligation. As life gets more frantic, however, there's a tendency to square off anything we can squeeze into our days without partners or family as 'me time'. Such as haircuts, doctor's visits and sick days. These are more essential than they are fun – and fun activities produce the best result.

Here are five essential strategies for carving out 'me time'.

1. Rate yourself.

Know you're worth spending time with – and on. That's the only way you will prioritise yourself – and your use of time.

Draw a pyramid and put yourself at the top of it. Then put all the people you love and care about in order underneath. (Don't show them this, it will only cause trouble.) The point is you matter most. Don't go visit Aunty Jill on Saturday when you want to go for a walk on the beach. Unless Aunty Jill is a riot and will take you out on the town for some fun. If you don't put some time and effort into yourself, you won't be in great shape to enjoy your relationship and/or your family.

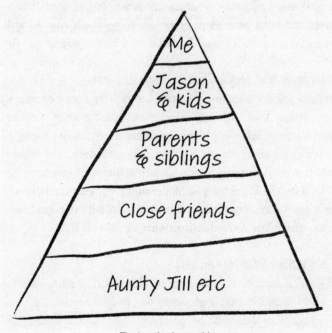

The 'me time' pyramid

2. Know what's fun for you.

When you get some time, know exactly what you want to do with it. 'Me time' can – and should – be exactly what YOU want it to be. Some people want to socialise, others like to sit alone in a movie theatre, while others have a massage, go fishing or brew beer. Pick what works for you and ask the people you love to help you find time for it.

3. You don't need heaps of time.

At times in our lives, we're Just. So. Busy. Don't aim for hours of 'me time' because you'll be left permanently discontented. Just make sure what you do is (1) *regular* and (2) *refreshing*.

4. Set boundaries and guard your time like a lion.

Make appointments with yourself and keep them. Don't bail on your plans as soon as someone demands something of you. When you diarise and keep your plans, your self-respect will rise. So will the respect others have for you. And that may be the biggest win of all.

5. Give rather than grab (or drop the points-scoring).

This is a sneaky one, but it works. Don't keep count of who's had what. When your partner wants time out for their interests or friends, encourage them wholeheartedly. Try to make it easy (well, as easy as possible) for them to go away guilt-free, and enjoy their time. If your partner is also a Good Partner – or trying to be one – they'll do the same for you. A giving vibe inside a relationship is better than a grabbing one – it creates goodwill all round.

Exercise: Answer the following:

- What do I do for myself?
  ....
- How much time (each week) do I dedicate to it?
  ....

- Am I satisfied with this? Yes/No
  ....
- How could I create time for me?
  ....
- How could I protect this time?
  ....

How to cope with guilt

In the 21st century, guilt is almost a bona fide psychological syndrome. The demands on us are relentless and we feel guilty about not getting them done, or that we should be doing more, having more and being more than we are. And that's before we even get to Big Picture guilt. All the sad and bad things other people down the road, around the country and across the globe are going through.

The guilt that really crawls under the skin is close to home; it's tied to partners and family, friends, work, health and our own potential. That guilt can make us unwell emotionally, showing up in symptoms of depression and anxiety, and often physically, too.

Women particularly struggle with guilt – mainly that they're not doing enough, or that they're trying to do too much and not making a good job of any of their roles or, worse than that, doing everything badly.

There are two types of guilt – acute and chronic – and they can feed into each other. For example, day-to-day feelings of guilt (acute) can fuel a belief that you're not a worthy person (chronic), and vice versa. Here's a definition of each with examples.

1. Acute guilt
This is related to what's going on in our world right now. *Shouting at the kids. Not showing for a friend's birthday. Not getting to the gym. Using the iPad to babysit the kids. Grabbing*

takeaway instead of cooking healthy, AGAIN. Blobbing in front of Netflix, AGAIN. Missing a deadline. Texting someone you shouldn't be texting.

2. Chronic guilt

A persistent belief that you've done (or are doing) something wrong. Certain factors may contribute to this: your family history, culture, religion, or a family member who uses power plays or 'guilt trips' you. Over time, chronic guilt fuels insecurity and negatively shapes our perception of ourselves. Having an affair. Not being able to control an addiction/letting your partner down. Not putting enough effort into your key relationships. Being a workaholic. Not being there for the kids/giving them enough opportunities. For separated or sole parents, trying to make up for a split or the absence of the other parent.

Guilt is a complex emotion that needs deeper exploration, especially the chronic variety. But we all need a starting point for lightening the load. Here are some strategies to combat it.

Call it out by naming it.

Guilt gives you that squirmy feeling in your stomach. Often, you're not quite sure where it's coming from. Giving it a name (like 'George') and saying out loud what you feel guilty about makes it real, and allows you to examine it for its validity. *Hey, George. It's you again. Should I really be beating myself up like this? Or this much?* Most often, the answer is 'no'.

Stop apologising.

If you've messed up, you need to own it and apologise to the right person. But domestic guilt often causes us to feel bad about all the things we're not doing – then spin in circles trying to make up for them. Before you launch into another round of 'sorry', stop and check yourself. If you're doing your best, that's enough.

Lower the bar you've set for yourself.

Have you set unrealistically high expectations of yourself? Let's say you want to get to the gym every day. Or visit your mother. But, given all your other commitments, it's an impossible task. Lower the bar to fit with your life. This is not about 'dumbing down' your expectations. It's better for you psychologically to achieve a smaller goal than to keep screwing up.

Set (and keep) boundaries.

Others often make us feel guilty for what we're not doing. But your time, your health and your partner/family are your priorities. Put boundaries around your time and what you do for others. And know this: to survive the maelstrom of life, you even need to set boundaries around what you do for your family. You need to save something of yourself for yourself.

Separate guilt from shame.

Guilt and shame are frequently poured into the same bucket, which makes us feel even worse. It's best to think of it like this: *guilt relates to 'bad behaviour', while shame is about being a 'bad person'*. I did something bad (guilt) versus I *am* bad (shame).

We all behave badly at times, but that doesn't mean we are bad people. So keep the things you've done wrong in the 'guilt' bucket and tell yourself that bad behaviour is permissible (and normal) as long as you don't keep repeating it.

Replace punishment with compassion.

If you've done what you need to do to atone for your mistake (such as apologise), then there is no need to stay in a prison of your own making. If you're in the habit of coming down hard on yourself, ease up. Don't punish yourself – show yourself compassion instead.

Couples and shared goals

Couples can benefit hugely from shared goals. These bind you together and make you feel like you're heading in the same direction, even when life feels overwhelming. You need to review and change your goals to align with changing circumstances.

Do you set goals with your partner? Seems like an easy aim, right? But when you ask couples if they have shared goals, you'll mostly be met with a blank, or nervous, stare.

Some will cough up plans for a mid-year holiday; others will start talking about financial goals – savings or retirement plans.

But ordinary, fun stuff for the sake of their relationship? Nope. When pressed, they mutter they might try to resurrect date night, or something. Or they might try to get a weekend away together during the year.

But there's nothing locked in.

Why should we?

Many people butt heads with the concept of long-term or even medium-term goal-setting. I get it: the longer you live, the more you realise that life has a funny (and often strange) way of derailing the best-laid plans.

But it's still worth making them. It's still worth trying to take charge of at least some aspects of your life, rather than casting it (entirely) to the winds of fate. And that includes your intimate relationships.

People do better psychologically when working towards something – even if it's stressful. Couples, too, function better when they're on the same page, working for the same ends. I've seen it happen; I've also seen the fallout when they don't.

If you're up for it, here's a five-step process for using goal-setting to enhance your relationship.

Shared goals: A five-step plan

1. Look back in wonder.

Well, maybe not wonder, but just look over your shoulder. We tend to measure ourselves forward, against what we want – what we haven't achieved yet. This can put us on the back foot, feeling like we're not doing enough. Or, worse, that other couples are doing better.

It's healthier and more of a psychological boost to note what you've already achieved together. You don't have to cover your whole relationship – that will make the exercise too onerous. Just stick to the past year. Every couple, even if they are in a rocky or conflictual place, will have done or learned something worthwhile. Praise it.

2. Identify the areas of your lives that most relate to you both.

Here are some examples: House and/or garden. Domestic projects. Money. Parenting/family. Couple time. Individual time. Holidays. Special events. Fresh activities. Work. Leisure. Sex. Work habits. Future.

Pick three – obviously, you can pick as many as you like, but beware of overwhelming yourselves if you're new to the game. Even one is a good start.

Brainstorm a specific goal in each of the three areas and, *when you've agreed on each goal*, write it down.

3. Stick to the three golden rules.

Goals must be specific to the 12 months ahead. Big, grand plans are fine but it's helpful to have some that keep you pinned down to the current year.

Your goals as a couple need to be measurable (so you can say whether they've been achieved or not). Even better, if you can measure progress during the 12 months – not just at the end of it.

At least one of your goals must be fun. Don't just load your list with heavy plans to reduce debt and lay gravel in the driveway (even if you love gravel). Make sure there's something on the list you can both look forward to.

4. Check the vibe the goals give you.
Sit with your list for a while and note your feelings about what's on it. Pursuing your goals should make you feel GOOD (not exhausted or stressed). If they don't make you feel good, or look like they will help you move forward together, adjust them.

5. Don't neglect yourself.
Not all your goals should be shared, nor should they all be chosen by your partner. It's important to have independent hopes and dreams within your relationship.

So think about yourself, too. Identify what YOU want from your year. Talk to your partner about it – and listen to his or her plans, too. Then figure out a way to make it happen, for both of you.

Load-sharing: Quick takeaways

- You're not alone: The chore wars are a universal struggle for couples.
- Emotional labour is hard to quantify – and harder to share. But it needs to be considered in the division of chores.
- Micromanaging is best left at the office.
- Perfectionism is exhausting. Everyone has a right to load the dishwasher their own way.
- It's better to give time than to grab it. But sometimes, you have to grab it.
- Sick days and doctor's visits are not 'me time'.
- There's no such thing as Over-Thanking.
- Couples do (much) better with shared goals.

PILLAR 6:
PLAY

How do you have fun?

'If you would read a man's Disposition, see him Game, you will then learn more of him in one hour, than in seven Years Conversation.'

– Richard Lingard

Why does it matter? Play includes leisure, social activities and fun. Sharing activities and having fun together creates positive emotions, which can strengthen your bond and help overcome any differences. While the phrase 'The couple that plays together, stays together' might be optimistic, it certainly helps.

***

When he said that having fun tells us more about ourselves than talk, the 17th century Irish priest and academic Lingard was talking about individuals. But it may be true of couples, too.

Good partners know how to play. Study after study shows that couples who 'play', have fun and enjoy each other's company have higher levels of positive interaction, which is a critical factor in long-term relationship satisfaction.

Playing, or having fun together, is probably underrated as a contributor to being a good partner. In trying to keep relationships afloat, it can seem like trust, communication and conflict skills are heavier hitters. But play increases bonding, improves communication and helps to manage conflict. If you peer into real life, it's the hallmark of many successful couples, provided the light mood is consistent, and not just the occasional laugh on the battlefield.

On a practical level, play counterpunches the heaviness of life. It saves us from the boredom of long-term togetherness, from night after night on the couch, from stresses about kids and money, from the relentlessness of dirty dishes, from the monotony of remembering to put out the recycling bin. It can also promote better sex. Playfulness in bed lightens the mood and decreases any anxiety. It is a means through which couples can deepen and personalise their relationship. It can be a way of feeling special and exclusive, enriching the connection between partners.

Not surprisingly, one of the biggest threats to play is work, primarily because it takes up so much time and energy. It can wind us up, wreck our health, even take over our identities, so when it goes badly, or ends, we're left wondering who we are. It can also curl its tentacles into relationships and families, causing conflict and disconnect.

Do you play well in relationships? Let's take a look at the importance of spending time together – and apart. First up, however, is a look at what happens when work grabs too much of the domestic pie. Over to Kiri.

All work and no play: Kiri's story

Kiri's love of work is sparking trouble in her relationship.

A high flyer in the financial world, she's risen steadily up the ranks and now holds a prestigious position in a large organisation. She puts in full days at work, drags the laptop out after dinner most nights and keeps up with the flood of emails at the weekend. She's also big on staff care, answering calls from her team and queries after hours.

Kiri and Billy have been together for 20 years. He was the primary caregiver of their two sons when they were young; it was a choice they made together, because she was more ambitious than him – and earned a lot more. 'Billy's always been great, hugely supportive of my work. It worked really well for a long time,' she says.

Now, their sons have left home, and Billy wants to spend more time with Kiri, socialising and sharing activities. He'd like to get away from the city more often, maybe even get a campervan and do some touring.

Kiri is having a hard time with that. 'I love to work,' she says. 'It's my happy place. I feel more stressed out when I'm not working, when I know things are piling up at the office.

'Billy says we need to spend more time together for the sake of our relationship, but I can't let go of work. Whenever I take time out, I feel antsy and guilty. We argue about it – it used to be a little, now it's a lot.

'Billy says I'm married to my job. He says I give the best of myself to work, that I need to have more work-life balance. It winds me up because my career – my salary – has given this family so much. We've never wanted for anything; we've had some great holidays. Now, when it suits Billy to slow down, he expects me to do so, too.'

She pauses, suddenly looking lost. 'I do feel guilty. Part of me knows what he says is true, but I don't know how to change it. I don't even think I want to.'

***

Kiri's struggle with work, and the tension it's causing in her relationship, is common to many couples. Work addiction is a key source of conflict – not just the amount of time it consumes, but the message it sends to a partner: that my work's more important to me than you. On top of that, having to hear about your partner's work stress and struggles, night after night, is extremely draining on a relationship.

It's likely that Billy's point of view is less about wanting to socialise or trip around in a campervan, and more about feeling valued by Kiri. Or at least more valuable than her direct report, who's taking up a chunk of Kiri's time because she's having some trouble in her own marriage. He probably also feels that, after raising the boys and working so hard for so long, they deserve a little fun.

But Billy doesn't say this. He's not great at expressing his feelings. Instead, he feels hurt and angry. He makes snide remarks about her never being around. He shoots down Kiri's love of work when he's always been proud of her achievements. And he lectures her about work-life balance, which essentially gets them nowhere.

Work-life balance – the equal prioritising of work and personal life – is still seen by many as aspirational. Like it's some kind of mirage in the desert we should be crawling towards because, when we get there, we'll all feel happier and healthier. But, as in Kiri's case, that's not always true. Work is where she feels at her best and most calm. She loves Billy but the idea of relaxing, of endless days travelling from sunset to sunset in a campervan, makes her feel ill.

Besides, work-life balance is an unrealistic goal in a world that often demands people work long hours just to keep their families and lifestyles afloat. Nor is it really what people want. We've just been tricked into thinking we do, because feeling exhausted makes us long for more leisure time. But it's not a balance we seek. We want to spend our time in worthwhile ways and feel a sense of pride, achievement and meaning in our work. Beyond that, what we long for is not about work. We want to be loved. We want to be seen and feel important to someone – but not always in a deep and serious way. We also want to have fun with them.

Play time: Why we need it

As Kiri and Billy were finding out, work can be tough on relationships and families. Beyond the time and energy drain, work scatters our attention; it makes us answer emails at the beach and in the park and late at night; and it causes partners and kids to feel invisible and unimportant. I can't count the number of clients who've told me they never really knew one or other of their parents, because they were always working, or they seemed to prefer work to engaging with their families. And it's got worse as work stress rises and technology makes it harder for us to get away from it.

On the other hand, I can easily count the number of people who've said their parents had lots of fun together or the mood at home was playful. That's understandable – the pressures of life and laundry tend to work against light-heartedness. But I also find it a little sad. Because surely, one of the foundation purposes of life is to enjoy it, or at least not to grind through every day with gritted teeth.

Play is supposed to be carefree, without purpose. This idea knocks up against our 21st-century obsession with productivity and efficiency, so it means we're constantly attaching our play to outcomes. We go to the gym to build muscle, improve cardio fitness or lose weight; we go on holiday to recover from work; we take our kids places that will expand their worldview; we even have sex because we should or to alleviate guilt. But being obsessed with outcomes and what others are doing, or how they're judging us, compromises our enjoyment.

While we can march through life making serious contributions to the Greater Good, it's worth remembering most of the stones we throw will barely cast a ripple. So, we might be better to focus our attention elsewhere – or at least ensure an even spread of it. Plenty of research reminds us about the importance of relationships in the grand scheme of things – not just romantic ones, but the people we spend time with. No-one on their deathbed frets about that 90-page report they never handed in. Or that toxic boss they had in their third move on the career ladder. Or even the professional awards they won or didn't. Instead, they reflect on the people in their lives – the good times they enjoyed with them, how much they loved and were loved back. If they have any regrets, it's far more likely to be about people loved and lost, than work.

Are you fun to live with?

Work took more than its pound of flesh from her, Kiri said. When she did take time off, she was often irritable and distracted, without much energy for leisure time. She wasn't up for much at the weekends, including sex: 'I've got little enough energy and peri-menopause takes the rest.' If she didn't have work to do on weekends, she built a nest into the couch and stayed there. She went to the gym three mornings a week because she put it in her calendar – and she wanted to halt the mid-life weight gain – and occasionally had a night out with her girlfriends. But, she admitted, Billy got the weary, cut-price version of herself.

My goal is never to make a client feel worse, so I asked her my favourite question. I think it's one we should have taped to our fridges because we all need reminding. And it's the one I always ask clients, because it forces you to experience how other people experience you.

Are you fun to live with?

She looked a little blank. 'I'm all right on a good day. A bit of a bitch sometimes. You'd have to ask Billy.'

There was no need to ask Billy because that would be cheating. This is a self-reflective exercise.

Good Partners strive to improve the home atmosphere. *What's your mood around the house?*

How to test if you're a fun partner (or the other kind)
Give yourself a tick for every 'Yes' answer.

❑ You're spontaneous.
❑ You greet your partner's suggestions with a 'yes' (or, if you really don't like the idea, you pause to think instead of slamming them with a 'no').
❑ You spend decent chunks of quality time with your partner away from your phone and devices.
❑ You can make your partner laugh, even if you've been together a while.
❑ You're good company – you can bring some lightness to the mood.
❑ You go with the flow, or even enjoy it, when thrown out of routine.
❑ You have ideas. You initiate things. AND you make them happen.
❑ You're playful with affection/sex.
❑ You're often on the lookout for fun, or things for the two of you to do.
❑ You're up for going to important events with your partner's friends and family (not skulking in the corner and being dragged along, kicking and screaming).
❑ You're not hypercritical and negative about other people (including your partner).
❑ You can have a great time without being drunk or high.

❏ You have healthy ways of managing your worries and stress.

❏ You don't always talk about how busy you are.

❏ You're not constantly complaining.

❏ You have good stories to tell (but you know when to stop telling them).

❏ Your vibe is generally upbeat.

❏ Your partner wants to do things with you.

How'd you go?

Hopefully, you got a whole lot more ticks than crosses on the test.

If not, cut yourself a break. No-one's life is the stuff of stand-up comedy. Everyone goes through bad days and faces challenges. Even just the great wash cycle of life can suck the spirit from us all. Getting through all you have to do every day can be hard, without having to be fun on top of it. I've had plenty of people challenge me on this. I accept it's not easy. As one woman said: *'I've already got so much to do, why do I have to be FUN as well? Isn't just being decent good enough?'*

Whoa, okay, good point. You can be whoever you want, as long as it works for the two of you. You don't have to be the life of every party, which raises an important point. Being playful is not about partying hard, which can promote another set of problems altogether! It's worth keeping an eye on your fun factor, however, because it affects your mental health and general life satisfaction. And hopefully, you've seen the message-behind-the-message here. Play helps to remind us of the upside of being alive. Being fun to live with isn't just for your partner's benefit. You are living with yourself, too.

How to avoid the 'boring partner' trap

Remember how it was at the beginning?

You couldn't wait to see your partner to share the day's news. But lately, the conversation has dried up. So has the sense of adventure. You wouldn't call it bad – just predictable, a little stale. *How was your day? What's for dinner? What's up with the kids? Who's doing the pick-ups tomorrow?*

You feel a niggle of discontent. Your life with your partner is boring. But, as you hit the Netflix button for the sixth night in a row, a random thought floats into your head.

Maybe that semi-conscious person in track pants on the couch next to me is thinking the same thing. *Maybe I'm boring to be with?*

It's a smart question. Before you file your relationship under Dry as Dust, it's worth turning the spotlight on yourself to see if the problem may lie – gulp – even closer to home than your partner.

Are you exciting or dull?
Here's a quiz to test yourself (answer 'yes' or 'no'). Do you:

1. Always greet your partner with 'How was your day?'
Okay, I don't want to be too tough on you. Asking *'How was your day?'* is better than no question at all. But seriously? You can do better than that for someone you love. Think about what's been going on for them and form a specific question around that.

2. Believe you're the Exciting One in the relationship? Or are you the Dull One?
Both of those beliefs are unhelpful in a relationship so, if you're clinging to either of those, it's time to let it go. I recall one client – a lovely, warm woman – who consistently pitched herself as the boring one, saying that her partner had all the charisma, all the ideas, all the popularity. She just lived in his shadow. I happened to meet this man and, after five minutes, was exhausted by him. He was less exciting than opinionated and it was hard to believe she felt inferior to him.

It's supposed to be a partnership into which two people bring their strengths AND their vulnerabilities. That means you should both get to shine – and be able to take a back seat – when appropriate.

3. Grab all the airtime?
True, one person may be more of a 'talker' than the other – but check you're both getting a fair opportunity to speak. One of you (the quieter one) may have hopes and dreams you haven't been able to express.

4. Say nothing at all?
Saying nothing – or shutting down – even if you are low in mood or struggling, puts a massive strain on relationships. It's important to contribute, to let your partner know what's up (or if there's a reason for your silence). Silence is unnerving in a relationship; it's important to make an effort.

5. Wish your partner were more like you (even if you don't say so)?
People often believe they'd be more content with someone more like themselves. That's not true, nor is it fair. Your partner should be as free to be who they are as you are. And you should appreciate the differences between you.

6. Complain a lot?
Even if you have good reason for complaining, like a high-stress job, constant negativity is hard to live with. So is hearing the same work-stress stories, night after night. If that rings a bell, try to back up the truck a little when you hear yourself start. If you have a particular stressor in your life, seek help for it, so your partner doesn't have to take all the load.

7. Always function as a creature of habit?

Take the same route, eat the same food and do the same things, day after day after day. While keeping things structured lowers anxiety, allows you to cope and provides a solid framework for your life, utter predictability can also feed boredom, both in yourself and in a relationship. Try to change things up a little. And, when you can, make a suggestion – initiate something.

8. Decline most invitations or your partner's suggestions?

Withdrawal from other people, social events, and life generally, is a symptom of depression. So if you find yourself doing this frequently – and especially if it is more than you used to – check in on your mental health and seek help if you need it.

9. Feel bored with life?

This feeling will snake through your relationships with your partner and any family you have. If you feel uninterested and unmotivated, take care not to lump all the blame on your partner. Maybe your life needs a reboot – or you need to spice things up for yourself? A new job? A fresh project? Take up a new interest? Meet more people? Join a community group? If this is you, begin now. Any form of change will give you more to bring to your relationship.

Results

Boring? If you noticed a sprinkling of 'yes' answers, you could do better. You can do lots of things to bring some colour, or even just a little intrigue, into your relationship. Start by making a change – anywhere.

If all your answers were 'no', why are you still here? Please take your riveting personality away to your wondrous relationship, so the rest of us can focus on improving ours!

How to increase your fun factor

Everyone is boring sometimes. Life can slip into humdrum routines, which isn't always a bad thing. We need routines to help us cope with all we have to do. And some down-time (or time doing nothing) can give our minds and bodies a much-needed break; it can fill up our tanks again, ready for the next thing.

Beware of too much repetitiveness in your relationship, however, because it leads to a slow (and sometimes subtle) disconnect. If left for too long, it's hard to light the fuse again. So make a plan. You don't have to rock the stand-up comedy routine, but you do have to try. Here are some ideas for bringing more play into your relationship.

Greet each other with (more) excitement.

'I'll feel like a fool,' one client said to this suggestion. True, she did at first, because it was a leap out of character. She was a low-key person who didn't get excited easily. But she tried it on her partner – with surprisingly positive results.

Check in on how you greet your partner and, if it's not 10/10, take it up a few notches. At the very least, it'll give you both a laugh. Seriously though, everyone responds well to being greeted with enthusiasm. Everyone wants to think others are happy to see them. Everyone gets a shot of pleasure from it. If you've ever had a dog, you'll know what I mean.

Change yourself up, physically.

Go to the gym, take a walk, dress up a bit, change your hair, change your shirt colour, wear weird jewellery, get some piercings or a tattoo, or make yourself look good or interesting or different or bold. Even if your partner doesn't notice, you'll give yourself a boost.

Find out what makes your partner happy (or happier).

Sounds obvious, I know, and if you've been together a while, you should know this. Maybe you're on board with the Big Stuff: you know they love skydiving and Italian food and lying in a hammock sipping on frozen margaritas. But do you know the little things? Start by finding out their favourite thing to do on an ordinary weekend then plan a way to make it happen for them. Hopefully, it'll include you. (And, if it doesn't, keep asking until you find something that does. You're paying, after all.)

Make a mini bucket list – instead of date night.

OMG, date night. It must be the most well-worn offering in romantic self-help. Having regular dates with your partner will help your relationship, but not if the thought makes you want to go to bed (alone with your book). Instead, create a list of fun things to do together. Keep adding to it. Aim to cross off 12 things every year – one for each month (e.g. trying a new/different restaurant, visiting a new suburb/town, taking a coastal walk, trying a new activity, seeing a movie you normally wouldn't). Or take turns to come up with a surprise.

Be sexually playful.

I know, after you've been with someone a while, you're not getting out the erotica deck when you get home. As renowned relationship expert Esther Perel says: 'Paris just isn't the same on your fifteenth trip as it was on your first.' The novelty factor skips town. In a very fast car.

It's commonly thought that good sex is always spontaneous, uninhibited and irresistible. But that's a myth, and unrealistic for most couples who've got beyond the honeymoon period. All couples go through periods when desire waxes and wanes, and sex is unsatisfying. It doesn't matter what kind of sex you have – hot, planned, utilitarian, slow, novel, unfinished, cuddles, a massage, sexy text messages, flirting – as long as it's not a duty or burden. Planned sex is fine, but dutiful sex isn't fun for anyone. Being sexually playful also isn't about engaging in your partner's unappealing suggestions. It begins with letting go of sexual expectations/outcomes and being more playful in your relationship and life generally. This playfulness will spill over into your sex life.

Shake up your weeknight routine.
Evenings during the week are when couples most frequently report the first niggles of boredom and discontent. That's when everything slips into the same-old, same-old zone. Do an inventory of how you spend your Monday–Thursday evenings. If they look all like replicas of each other, resolve to shake things up a bit. Do at least one thing differently. Starting tonight.

Don't be the one always at home, waiting.
Even if you love being home, don't sit by the heater in your slippers every night, waiting for your partner to come home. Go out sometimes. Try a new activity. Put on sneakers instead of slippers – anything. Be reliable, but don't be utterly predictable in your habits. It'll make you dull – even to yourself.

Reflect on the good times.
Every relationship has its 'ups'. The trouble is, when we hit a flat patch, we default to the 'downs'; it can be hard to remember the good times. Use photos, music, books, holiday memories as prompts. Or just involve your partner in finishing these sentences: 'We had great fun when we …' 'Do you remember that time we …?' With a little creativity, you may be able to re-create those feelings.

Do something nice you wouldn't normally do.
If you always do nice things for your partner, don't stop. If you never do nice things, however, this will (sadly) be easy for you.

Either way, take a jump to the left. Do what you don't – or you wouldn't – normally do. It's the easiest way to be noticed.

Laugh – it's the secret sauce of great relationships.

I'm not talking about either of you running side-splitting gags 24/7. To be fair, when you're both up to your necks in life stress, it can be pretty hard to tap anyone's funny bone. But research shows that humour positively influences relationship satisfaction. As long as the humour is genuine – not the aggressive, sarcastic, belittling kind.

When asked what people look for in a mate, nearly everyone cites humour. They'll often rank it higher than more obvious choices, such as intelligence and independence. (One man I worked with put it before personal hygiene. He was single. Just saying.) Here's the interesting thing, though: nearly everyone hopes they're also funny; that they can make their partner laugh.

The research is divided: some studies indicate it's not essential to have the same sense of humour as your partner, as long as you find some middle ground. But common sense suggests that finding the same things funny is more helpful than not.

Laughter can be tonic for your relationship. It can help to reduce stress levels, dilute conflict, make you feel like you're on the same page as one another, and can bind you as a couple with all the little in-jokes you share. More broadly, it raises the spirits: laughter is what makes the world spin. Genuine laughter makes us feel better about everything. While laughter may not fuel hope, it may be the beginning of it. And it certainly lights up any moment. Whether you have a partner or not.

Playing together versus playing alone

While playing together is important in a relationship, so is time to 'play alone' – to be by yourself or with your own friends and/

or indulging in your own interests. (Note: You should distinguish Playing Alone from Playing Away, for obvious reasons.) Having time away from your partner can recharge you and bring back a freshness to the relationship. As well as giving you other things to talk about, having your own life means you're not relying on your partner to meet all your needs.

It's a commonly held belief that your partner needs to be your best friend. It's great if you feel that way, but your partner doesn't have to be your Everything. Expecting your partner to fulfil all your needs can put your relationship under a lot of pressure. One young woman wanted a partner to meet her intellectual, emotional, social, domestic, holiday, spiritual, sexual and leisure needs. She ran the list then sat back, looking surprised. 'I don't think that person exists. No wonder I'm single.'

While she was being hard on herself, it was a useful reflection. Different people meet different needs in us, and it's fine to find a balance that works for you.

It's worth remembering, too, that trouble can brew when you don't get the balance right – spending either too much time together or too much time apart. Let's take a look at each scenario.

Togetherness: Too much of a good thing

Most couples fall into one of two camps. Either they're fighting to get more time with their partners, or they're trying to have more time away from them.

Some couples are acutely aware that their love for each other, and their lifestyle, has a strong ring of reliance to it. They don't have much of a life outside coupledom. This is generally not a problem until things go wrong, or one or the other of them is left on their own. One couple I worked with had a business together. They spent all their free time together – movies, hiking, mountain biking – and they took all their holidays together, mostly in a bus they had converted into a tiny home on wheels. There was literally no space for anyone else, physically or emotionally, even if they wanted it. Then Al got sick with a terminal health condition, which was going to slowly reduce his capacity for activity. Suddenly, Lou was faced with the prospect of having to move into the caregiver role and, ultimately, realise he wouldn't be around forever. It had thrown her, psychologically, and that's when they booked in for some help.

When I gently introduced the idea of creating space for other friendships, Lou looked terrified. 'I've never been one for girls' weekends. I've never needed that. I've always just wanted to be with Al. He's my best friend.' Then the kicker: 'My life will be over if I lose him.'

Lou and Al had always bound their lives tightly together, even more so since their son had left home. They leaned on each other, physically, emotionally, and for support and security. Their identity was more 'Lou and Al' than individuals, and it seemed it would be difficult for either of them to function independently.

Couples who are unhealthily close emotionally are referred to as 'co-dependent' (reliant on a partner to meet their emotional needs or make them happy) or 'enmeshed' (responsible for each other's feelings). I don't rush to use those words, however, because it implies dysfunction. Lou and Al were not dysfunctional people; they'd just shaped their lives around each other. While they were both happy and healthy, there'd been no need to change the arrangement; it was only when Al got sick that they needed to address it.

In relationships that are unhealthily close, boundaries get blurred and emotions get hooked together so each feels the other's ups and downs intensely. This can happen in intimate relationships, but it can also show up between parent and child when they become over-involved in each other's lives.

These are the signs that you and your partner may be too close – or heading that way – followed by some strategies for helping you step back.

- Your self-worth is tied to your relationship and what your partner thinks of you.
- Your happiness depends on your partner's mood and emotional state.
- You neglect other relationships to be with your partner (or manage/hide their issues).
- You hate conflict between the two of you and will go to great lengths to avoid it.
- You feel lonely – or anxious – without your partner.
- You lose sight of what you like to do independently.
- You don't say 'yes' to ANYTHING without checking in it's okay with your partner.
- You absorb your partner's feelings. When your partner's unhappy, you are too. And when they're up, you're up.
- Whatever your partner needs or wants to do, you say 'yes'.
- You lose sight of, and investment in, separate interests and friends.

It can be hard to admit you're in an unhealthily close or enmeshed relationship with your partner because you see it as a weakness – and you may be too scared to change it. Being in such a relationship doesn't necessarily mean you have a poor sense of self or low self-worth. Plenty of strong, smart people have landed here. That's because this kind of change beds in slowly, and it can be hard to recognise when the relationship has crossed the line into something unhealthy.

All relationships need a little air for good health. My client Lou didn't have a dysfunctional relationship with Al. She was facing a difficult time with his declining health and she wanted to be there for him. She also recognised, for her own sake, it was time to take baby steps in a different direction. And he recognised it, too.

Here are some strategies to help:

Consider what you like to do, and your partner doesn't.
This may be a challenge if you're used to doing everything together; you may even have forgotten about some of your own or earlier interests. Even if you're close, there will be something. Spend some time brainstorming. What have you previously done and enjoyed? What have you always wanted to try?

Enrol in a class/course.
Make it easy to pursue a new interest by taking a class or enrolling in a course. It's easier to turn up to something formal – especially when you've pre-paid. Try to choose something where you have to show up in person, rather than online. It's a little more confronting but you'll feel courageous when you do.

Take yourself on a regular solo date.
Begin with something simple – a wander around an art gallery or a day trip to the movies (lots of people fly solo at the movies). Slowly, get comfortable with being out on your own.

Say 'yes' to an invitation to go out without your partner.
Again, keep it simple. If it's stressful for you, don't stay for too long.

Stop trying to fix your partner's problems.
Couples who are too close will often rush in to solve their partner's problems. Step back a little and let them come up with their own solutions. Remember: support – but don't carry. Keep a lid on the advice. You'll be doing them a favour, too.

Love is leaving your partner alone sometimes.
Give your partner a chance to get to know themselves and what they're interested in, too. Encourage them to do things without you.

High independence: Too much time apart

One woman I worked with wanted to spend more time with her 'highly independent' partner. But he was hard, if not impossible, to pin down.

'He says he loves me, but it's like he doesn't need me,' she said, describing his behaviour as a little detached, almost as if he wasn't in a relationship with her.

'I try to discuss it with him, but I just end up feeling needy – even desperate. What should I do?'

Western culture prizes independence. We're fed the idea that high self-reliance – the ability to think and act for yourself – is the key to creativity, success and being the person you want to be.

In intimate relationships we're encouraged to hold tight to our independence, keep up with our friendships and interests, and nurture our own sense of self.

All of which is fine. BUT ... successful relationships require *healthy levels of emotional dependence* – being there for each other emotionally – so we can offer, ask for and accept support when it's needed.

That can be difficult to achieve when one of you values independence over everything else.

There are many reasons why highly independent people function this way. They may have a problem with intimacy, which tracks back to childhood, when they failed to develop secure attachments with their parental figures. They may also have suffered loss, rejection or betrayal, or have been emotionally traumatised/unwell.

Other reasons include being 'married' to their work, friends, mountain bike or golf clubs (code for other interests). Or still being emotionally attached to a previous partner. Or having been single for a long time.

Key signs of high independence

If you are with someone who is highly independent, or if you function this way yourself, you will probably recognise most of these signs. These are not an index, they are just designed to give you an idea of this type of function.

- They need A LOT of alone time. Or time with their friends.
- They struggle to express emotion easily or ask for support.
- They avoid 'emotional conversations' – including saying what's going on for them.
- They are extremely career-focused, or spend a lot of time doing their own interests.
- They are uncomfortable with comforting you (even when they are willing).
- They give the impression they're fine without a partner.
- They can be hard to pin down for time together because they usually have a full schedule (or they like to keep options open).
- You often feel like you need more from them (when this is not a pattern for you).

***

When you're with a person who functions so independently, it's easy to feel rejected or like you're not a priority for them. These feelings are valid. Before you bail out, however, do some research and check your own place in it. The only decision you have to make is whether you can find some middle ground with them and – ultimately – whether it will work for you. Here are some ideas to guide you.

Don't take it personally.

Take yourself out of the equation. It's important to know that how your partner operates is rooted in *their* inter-relational style – not yours. Adopt an open approach, as you figure out whether this relationship works for you.

Find out if there's a reason.

You don't want to rush in as a full-on detective too early, but frequently, people have valid experiences with loss that handbrake their ability to be intimate. So, when the time is right, see if you can find out what has led to this, and whether your partner knows it and is willing to work on it.

Give them space.

A highly independent person desperately needs space for their own equilibrium and mental health. If it's lost or taken away, they'll be unhappy and likely to back away. Encourage them to see friends and maintain their interests, and keep space for your own interests and friends, too.

BUT ensure you're a high priority in your partner's life.

This can be tricky – especially in the early stages, and if they have kids or family demands. Don't hang at the bottom of their list because of it. In an established relationship, make sure that you can count on your partner, that they make time for you and will be there for you when you need them. Most of all, make sure they VALUE you.

Ensure you can spend time on your own happily.

This doesn't mean you have to totally support yourself within a relationship – that's not a partnership. It does mean you should be able to enjoy your own company and manage your own emotions when you're on your own. Accept that if you need a great deal of emotional support in a relationship, this person might not be right for you.

Put yourself first (or don't make excuses for your partner).
Consider what you need from a relationship and a partner. Ask yourself how *you feel when you're around him/her*. Not just on a good day, but when you're hanging out.

If you find yourself constantly making excuses for their failure to prioritise or support you: their crazy busy job, their love of sports, their devotion to their kids, their terrible past, their controlling father, their mother's moods ... let's just say the warning lights are flashing.

Play: Quick takeaways

- How we play tells us who we are.
- No-one worries about an incomplete 90-page report on their deathbed.
- Your partner shouldn't have to meet ALL your needs.
- But you should be a top priority in the relationship.
- You CAN have too much of a good thing. Time apart is important too.
- Your boredom isn't (necessarily) your partner's fault.
- Laughter is the best medicine – except when medicine is.
- Being fun to live with is not just for your partner – it'll help your life, too.

Do you do the little things?

'We should give as we would receive, cheerfully, quickly and without hesitation; for there is no grace in a benefit that sticks to the fingers.'

– Seneca

Why does it matter? Kindness is the bottom line for care, consideration and understanding. It fosters goodwill, stability and satisfaction in a relationship.

***

Are you a kind partner? Most people bristle a little at that question. *Of course, I'm kind*, you think, silently wracking your brains for supporting evidence and hoping you won't be called to give it publicly. *Does yelling at the kids only once yesterday count? Or putting the rubbish out before being nagged into it? Or emptying the dishwasher even though it wasn't my turn?*

Kindness is having a moment around the globe. Okay, it's never been out of style but in a world that frequently seems harsh, unfair and full of prejudice, kindness wears an aspirational halo. We all want to be kind. We also want to be SEEN as being kind. Or at least to not be seen as whatever the opposite of kind is.

But are we *really* kind? In the rush of life, do we even have time to be kind? Are we kind where (and with whom) it matters most? Because if we were, it'd prevent a lot of heartbreak.

Kindness is the final pillar of love, even though it's managed to squirm into most of the others in one way or another. Last does not mean least – far from it. Kindness in relationships is hard to beat. Kindness (through thoughtful acts) is a practical way of showing love; kindness (of the reciprocated kind) has the power to transform relationships. Out in the world, it makes its mark, too. Research suggests that the more someone witnesses or receives kindness, the kinder they will be themselves. More than that, generosity is contagious – a single act can influence dozens more. So it makes sense that it will enhance every relationship it touches.

Kindness is frequently cited as the secret to healthy love. That when relationships fail, you'll see a breakdown in kindness. That two people who are kind to each other, even when stress and distraction pile up, have the best chance of staying together happily. That a relationship built on kindness is generous, with both partners focused on sharing freely, giving more than taking.

Kindness isn't about never being angry; it's about choosing how you express your anger, so you don't end up sending your relationship up in smoke. It's also about being generous about your partner's *intent*; in other words, giving them the benefit of the doubt. So a toilet seat left up isn't an act deliberately aimed at pissing you off, so to speak, it's just forgetfulness, born of distraction.

The trouble is, life *is* busy; we *do* get pissed off. We don't have time to step back and consider the intent behind our partner's failure to help out or be considerate. We just get mad – and resentful. And being resentful is an antidote to kindness; over time, it evaporates it. For proof, let's hear from Nik and Evie.

When kindness dries up: Nik and Evie's story

Nik and Evie came to therapy in a last-ditch hope for saving their dying relationship. They sat together on the couch, holding hands, looking bereft. They argued over everything, they had grown increasingly distant, and he had moved into the spare room.

'We've completely lost our way,' one of them said. The other nodded. 'If we don't do something quickly, it's over.'

As is usual for me, I saw them both together, then had an individual session with each to gather their perspective and a little of their history. These sessions are illuminating; some people speak and behave quite differently when they're on their own. It's also a good opportunity for the quieter partner to state their case.

When they came back together, things were no better. I noted that, in the four sessions we'd had, neither of them had said they loved each other. Not even in a friend-zone way. Not even that they once had. (For the record, that's quite telling. Even couples who are at war will still often say they love each other.)

There was no kindness between them. They had largely kept their conflict away from their young kids, but they operated in a tit-for-tat zone, where each good deed was a payback for something they owed, or a way of racking up credit they could use later.

They were well down the separation road. I made some suggestions, but they were sceptical. It seemed as if both of them had already made their decision, but were reluctant to say so because that would make it real. When I asked what they'd hoped to get from therapy, Evie shrugged and said sheepishly, 'Perhaps we were hoping you could save us?'

I wish. Sadly, no therapist has that kind of power, especially when both parties are resigned to separation. It's hard to watch two people who have bound their lives together call time on their relationship, especially when they're distressed about what it will mean for their kids.

In a situation like this, when they both had one foot already out of the relationship and the other foot raised and ready to run, there's probably no going back. All you can do is help them make sure they're sure that this – separation – is what they really want. And, if they do, help them do it as well as they can.

So I asked them to do one thing: to spend a month being as kind to each other as they could, no questions asked. The idea was to see if they could rekindle any goodwill. When they returned, they said it had made a difference. Focusing on giving rather than getting (or what they weren't getting) was helpful.

They eventually split up anyway – sorry, no Hollywood ending here, they were too far down the road of no return – but both said kindness had made a difference. The whole atmosphere of the house lifted.

'We get on better than we had for a long time,' Evie said. Nik agreed. 'We just wish we'd tried it years ago.'

Connecting through kindness

One of the ways we can promote kindness in our relationships is to be on the lookout for our partner's efforts to connect – and respond to them. As touched on in the Communication pillar, relationship expert Dr John Gottman calls these acts 'bids for connection'. If you can master your response to these bids, it's a superpower.

The thing is, however, our partners often don't make it obvious when they're wanting to connect. They don't stroll up and say, 'Hey, I'd like to connect with you,' or 'Let's share a moment together.' They just do something vague like tell a story from their day then get hurt when we don't look up from our phones.

A while back, my husband walked around a motel room we were staying in, making comments about several things he saw. When I didn't reply, he complained I wasn't listening to him. I'd been writing this book, so I recognised these comments as 'bids for connection'. I knew I was supposed to turn towards them and say something that made him feel whole and valued and special. But I was tired; I just wanted to sip my wine and stare into the void. Besides, I suspected these comments weren't genuine bids for connection; he was just being boring. So I said so. Gently, I hoped, but it didn't quite land that way. He did concede, however, that his 'bid for connection' was far from magnetic. So I got away with it.

The point is, it's pretty easy to not be kind, to not respond enthusiastically to every sentence that drops from our partner's lips. Because, honestly, we all talk our share of trivia. We all find our own 'stuff' more interesting than others do and we can all be a bit boring. But if we ignore our partners repeatedly – if we don't make regular efforts to respond and connect – resentment and ill will can quietly build up.

The important thing to remember is that 'bids for connection' contain messages. And what we do with those messages has a significant impact on our relationships. Here are some common examples of ways your partner might try to connect.

Verbal messages
- 'How was your day?' (*Designed to sound like it's about your day, but it's often more that they'd like to talk about theirs.*)
- 'Sharlene [from work] was a real bitch to Tim [from work] today.' (*Extremely boring when you have never met either of them.*)

- 'Wow, look at that Lambo!' (*Hard to respond when you don't like cars much and the car in question has already gone past.*)
- 'What do you think of [insert item from news media]?' (*Fair question, as long as it is not something of interest only to them.*)

Physical messages

- Stretching, yawning, sighing, emphasising pain in neck/ shoulder. (*Wanting empathy or a massage.*)
- Sending emojis or links to interesting stories. (*Fine, if you have time to look and they are actually interesting to you.*)
- Sending a text message just to see how you are. (*Great, so long as you don't get into trouble for not replying immediately.*)
- Touching the other person. (*Hopefully not just for sex.*)
- Pouring them a drink and sitting beside you. (*Wanting to talk – hopefully about your day as well as theirs.*)
- Doing a chore for you and hoping you'll notice. (*Lovely, as long as it's not done passive-aggressively.*)

The message often comes flagged as *I'm thinking about you.* And that may be true. But it's often also a poorly packaged cry for attention. The success of your relationship often depends on whether you turn towards them, blank them or turn against them.

Gottman outlines three key responses, to which I've added my own spin.

1. **Turning in.** You listen and absorb what's going on, and respond appropriately and lovingly. This is top-drawer kindness. A+ if you manage this consistently because almost no-one does.

2. **Turning away.** I call this blanking. Not (or barely) responding to your partner's bids. For example, nodding vaguely or grunting. While not generally ill-intended, you don't really hear them or pick up on their effort to connect. Hugely common between couples in a highly distractable world. If you do this often, you'll send back the message that your partner isn't interesting/important enough to you. Or that your work, phone, social media post or Netflix episode is more so.

3. **Turning against.** Responding negatively (especially if you do this to all their suggestions). Responding in a dismissive, critical, sarcastic or hurtful way. This has clear, and negative, implications for the future of any relationship.

Which way do you turn?

Unless you're super-human, you won't consistently turn towards your partner. We all get distracted, immersed in our own stuff or caught in our own heads. But it's worth thinking about how often you blank your partner with your vagueness. Or if you snap or criticise them when they don't deserve it. Which sentence best describes you?

❑ I mainly turn in.
❑ I mainly turn away.
❑ I mainly turn against.
❑ I wouldn't have a clue – I think I miss most of the hints.

There's no need to record an answer, especially if you want to pass this book on, but give it some honest thought.

The key thing is to be aware – notice – when your partner is trying to connect with you. Even bringing your attention to it can foster better communication. And responding with kindness – or conveying interest – is balm for your relationship. If you and your partner discuss this, you don't even have to be subtle. You can say, 'I'm making a bid for connection here,' so they don't have to guess.

When kindness is overcooked

Can you be too kind in a relationship? Part of me wants to say 'no', just to encourage people to be kinder. But I can't. It's possible that an overdose of kindness can undermine the health of a relationship – particularly when it's one-sided.

There are several ways you can be 'too kind', which can limit your partner's growth, but also have a detrimental effect on your own wellbeing and ability to live your own life. If you're a kind and giving person, it can be a real trap, because you're naturally inclined to 'do more'. And if you're a parent, it's difficult to get the balance right between doing too much for your kids and allowing them to grow up independently.

Below are the most common signs of being 'too kind'. Hopefully, you can rule out most of them for your partner and any kids you have. But, if not, it'll show you what you need to keep an eye on.

Thinking you know what's best for them

Maybe you do, but people have a right to make their own decisions, even if they're bad ones. This is particularly hard for parents when they see their kids heading down 'the wrong track'. My oldest daughter has a saying: 'Let me live, Mum, let me live,' when I have, let's call it, 'too much input' into her life. It's a fair call. Gentle suggestions are okay, but your partner (and kids) need to live – and mess up – all by themselves.

Having too many checks and controls

Constantly asking if your partner has eaten, checked their diary, has their keys/security pass, taken their meds, is warm enough, is taking a coat, etc. This is well-meaning, but you need to let your partner function independently. Or learn to. Treating them like a child will foster a lack of dependence. If you find yourself saying your partner is 'like having another kid', then you might need to pull back a bit. Actually, you definitely do. For your sake, as well as theirs.

Being too positive

Optimism is a good thing. It's protective against tough times. Excess positivity is just annoying, however, and can also undermine another person's struggles.

The 'toxic positivity' movement serves to dump on being positive as the expense of showing vulnerability. It's a valid suggestion because it's important to be real with feelings and give people space to express them. Personally, I like to save the word 'toxic' for things that are really poisonous.

Trying to please everyone

People-pleasing generally means that you're trying to be all things for all people. That's a fine motive. But in the end, it'll just make you feel tired, taken advantage of, and resentful. Learning to say 'no' is important for your health and relationship satisfaction.

'Fixing' their problems

It is kind to want your partner's life to be better. But rushing in and fixing all their problems isn't the way to do it. Not only will you fail to achieve this, but you'll stunt the development of their problem-solving skills. Allowing them to struggle and fail (within reason) will also give them moments of triumph when they solve a problem or rise again. And it will help build their resilience – and your respect in them.

Never disagreeing with them

Avoiding all conflict isn't kind, it's passive. Maybe even passive-aggressive. It's fine to want to keep the peace, but not if you don't have a voice in the relationship. Avoiding conflict is understandable if you have a controlling partner. But if you do, then the relationship may not be a good (maybe even a potentially unsafe) place for you to be.

Being over-protective

Over-protecting your partner can feel like kindness, but it can also be about your own need to keep control. It can also make them feel you don't trust them. Life is risky and you have to let your partner take some of those risks. Take note if your partner is too controlling of you and your activities: it's not healthy.

Generosity burnout: When you give too much

Are you one of life's 'givers'? You like to help people, brighten their day, lighten their load or promote their learning. It gives you pleasure to help, too, just like the research says.

But lately, you've begun to feel tired. Not just a bit worn – but soul-sucking fatigued. Your normal good humour has taken a hike. In its place, you feel an unfamiliar beat of resentment.

It's all give, give, give. Where's it going to end? When is someone – anyone – going to do something nice for me?

Givers will keep giving, even when they're running on empty. They'll sacrifice their own needs – such as eating well, exercise and friendships – to look after others or do the right, selfless thing. But when it lands on empty, you need to be careful. It's easy to slip into the red-light zone for burnout which, unchecked, can blow out into depression.

Generosity burnout is an occupational hazard in the caring professions, such as nursing and other healthcare, teaching and social work, but it also shows up in stretched families, where members have high needs or one person is carrying the heaviest load.

More broadly, anyone who works hard, is charged with (or wants to) help, or support others and struggles to say 'no' can fall victim to burnout.

The three key signs to watch for are:

1. **Exhaustion you can't shake.** Constant physical and mental exhaustion that even the weekend fails to refresh. People often report not wanting to get out of bed, feeling like they have nothing left to give. You feel pulled in too many directions, like you can't get off the conveyor belt.
2. **Feeling detached from and cynical about the people you're helping.** Where you once enjoyed helping and spoke well of the people in your world, you've begun to withdraw from them. You speak negatively about their needs, feel irritable, snap at people you like or love, and feel rising resentment every time someone needs you.
3. **Feeling ineffective, giving brings no pleasure.** People often report feeling like they're underperforming or failing on all fronts – at home, at work, or in their families and friendships – even though others don't notice. Take particular note when you start getting no joy from helping others. Anything you do feels mechanical.

If you find yourself in this place, here are some helpful ideas.

Know you're a good person.
Only kind, decent people struggle with generosity burnout. Yes, you might tend to over-seek approval or struggle to say 'no', but

you wouldn't get here if you didn't have a giving heart. So celebrate your goodness – just know you need to put some boundaries around it.

Take your feelings seriously.

Physical and mental exhaustion is a precursor to depression – don't ignore it and tell yourself it will come right with time. You might manage to patch yourself up, but only until the next time it all becomes too much. Take some time (and consider getting help) to figure out how you can make a change. *What can you pass over to others? What can your own people do to help?*

Say 'no' to all extras for a month.

Trim your life back to its simplest state. Do only what you have to do (for a generous person, even that will be a lot!) and say 'no' to absolutely everything else. Be clear, too (*I'm sorry, I can't do that*; *No, but thank you for the opportunity*), which closes down the request. If you leave the door open (*I'll do it if I can, I'll see how I get on*), you won't feel any relief. And the requests will keep coming.

Be a proactive giver (not the other kind).

There's a difference between *proactive giving* (where you decide what you want to offer, and which is healthy) and *reactive helping* (which is often prompted by the demands of others; it leads to feelings of resentment and will burn you out). Try to keep your giving on your terms – it's easier to manage and will give you more pleasure.

Don't be tricked into thinking you're special.

You are special, of course. But generous people aren't asked to do things because they're special. They're asked because they'll say 'yes'. The weird and slightly sad thing is that if you say 'no' firmly, the person asking won't care, they'll quickly move on to the next target. They're unlikely to care about your burnout either. So don't be fooled. When you're feeling exhausted, focus on doing things for people who genuinely value your contribution. And that's all.

Only give your one true thing (don't give up on giving).

Giving is good and it's good for us – we all know that – but not when it gets out of control. Not when your generous nature is compromised. When you're ready to get back in the game, pick your favourite thing to give – maybe you like to bake, do physical labour, write newsletters, make meals for older people, or give a few hours at the homeless or animal welfare shelters or a charity shop – and just do that. Pick and choose. For your health – as well as your sanity.

Kindness: The dysfunctional zone

Moving up a level, kindness can be at the base of some unhealthy relationship behaviours. Here are three case studies to illustrate – and strategies to help if they ring true to you.

- The Halo Effect: Loving your partner more than they love you
- Being a 'rescuer' in your relationships: Are you investing too much?
- Enabling: Are you helping your partner to hurt you?

The Halo Effect: Loving your partner more than they love you

Relationships are not perfectly and evenly formed.

That's because the people in them are, well, just people. It makes sense that we don't necessarily love in equal measure; one partner in a relationship is often more devoted than the other.

I recall one woman who couldn't stop talking about her husband. He was so charming, tall, handsome and funny; he looked so hot in a suit; everyone loved him; he could light up a room; he was such a good cook; and so socially skilled, she was so lucky to have him ...

Trust me, the list was long. When I saw a gap, I took it. 'But what about you?' I asked. 'Is he lucky to have you?'

She paused. Blinked. Shrugged. 'I don't really think about that.'

Welcome to the Halo Effect.

The Halo Effect is a cognitive or thinking bias, in which we're heavily influenced by our idealised views of someone. In the simplest terms, if we believe a person is great, we'll think whatever they do is great (even when it's not).

The Halo Effect is common in marketing, but it also has interesting implications for relationships. If you 'put a halo' on your partner, you'll see the good in everything they do. While that can promote harmony, it can also blind you to their flaws and lead you to justify poor behaviour. It can also cause you to see yourself as inferior.

There's nothing wrong with adoring, and wanting to please, your partner – as long as it doesn't come at the expense of yourself. In meeting your partner's needs, striving towards their goals and dreams, you can slowly lose sight of yourself. This means you can end up not knowing who you are as a person in your own right.

When this happens (or ideally, well before it does), it's time to back up the truck and redress the balance. It's never too late to find and express yourself as an individual.

Here come signs you may be too much of a 'pleaser' in your relationship, followed by some things to keep in mind. Note: These signs aren't necessarily signs of an unhealthy relationship, just that you may need more balance.

- You find yourself apologising to your partner more than you should.
- You always 'go with their flow' when they suggest activities.
- You pretend to agree with them to keep them happy.
- When they hurt your feelings, you don't say anything.
- You give up all your time for your partner (and family), even at the cost of your own health.
- You tend to adopt the views/interests of your partner.
- You find it hard or stressful to say 'no' to them.
- You always wear what they like you to wear (this is okay if it's what YOU love to wear, too).
- You find it easy to give compliments but hard to receive them.
- You're always trying to anticipate their needs.
- If they are unhappy, you feel responsible.
- You crave time to yourself but, in reality, you find it hard to get pleasure from your own choices.

What can you do?

1. Your partner is just a person.

They're no better than anyone else – and certainly not better than you. They are vulnerable and flawed in their own ways. Make sure you see their imperfections, too. Just as they don't need constant ego stroking, they don't need the pressure to be *amazing*. In putting a halo on someone, you're telling them they're the best they can ever be. They're not: It's healthy for everyone to be given room to change and grow.

2. You're training your partner in how to treat you.

When we begin a relationship, we're negotiating the other person's landscape – their thoughts, feelings, behaviour and history. We're trying to get a 'read' on them, work out the lumps and bumps, and figure out how to walk alongside each other successfully. How you treat yourself is important, because it guides your partner as to how you expect and want them to treat you. If you position yourself as inferior, think about the message you're sending out. *You are more important than I am.* Is that what you want?

3. Know what YOU bring to the relationship.

This is challenging for people who struggle with low self-esteem. In this case, my client was a lovely person, a devoted wife and mother; she had brought a huge amount to her marriage and family, and made a lot of sacrifices. When asked, she was dismissive about her role and input. She said, 'It's just what I do.' While that's true, you're allowed to – and need to – appreciate yourself within the relationship. Even more than that, you must.

4. Don't dodge the praise – welcome it.

Anyone who is in the habit of deflecting attention away from themselves will find it hard to take praise. They'll brush aside compliments or thank-yous or anything that builds them up – but be quick to absorb (and be hurt by) words or actions that bring them down. And this fosters low self-worth. So allow yourself to be praised/thanked: notice it and accept it graciously. When people know you appreciate it, they'll do it more often.

5. Name what lights YOU up.

People who've been giving a lot within their relationships or families often say they've lost their identity: *I'm not sure who I am anymore. I need to get back to me.* Having free time can make them feel anxious and insecure because they don't know what they want/like to do. So write yourself a list of your interests – including those you had in the past and would like to revive. Just seeing it written down gives you a starting point for reclaiming your identity.

6. Put the relationship first – not the person.

Relationships work best when each person acknowledges the importance of the partnership AND each believes they are making a valuable contribution. So prioritise your relationship – the needs of you BOTH rather than those of one partner. Create time to be together, to do things you both enjoy. Make sure your partner knows that they matter. And, if you want their full respect, show them you matter too.

Being a 'rescuer' in your relationships: When you're investing too much

Let's say your partner is a great person. They've had a tough start in life, they're a little damaged, they have a few difficulties they need to 'sort' and when they do, they'll have so much to offer.

They've been unlucky. They haven't had the right support, so far. But now? They have you. *You believe in them.* And you can help them fulfil their huge potential.

Does that story sound familiar? If so, you've probably taken the 'rescuer' role in your relationship. The first time it happens, it may just mean you're a decent person and supportive partner.

But if it becomes a pattern? Take note. Because being a 'rescuer' carries a high emotional price tag. And the one paying it is YOU.

Showing support and empathy is part of a healthy relationship. But how do you know when it's gone too far – that you've slipped into the 'rescuer' role?

Here are the key signs of being a 'rescuer' in relationships:

- You're often drawn to partners who are troubled or needy.
- You feel worthwhile when you help troubled people.

While this can be normal (and nice), rescuers often hook their self-esteem to providing this support.

- You over-invest in them – financially, emotionally, domestically and just taking the load off them.
- You go out of your way to protect them from emotional hurt or other people's critique.
- You (slowly) start micromanaging their lives to help them (e.g. organising them, helping them set up a diary, writing them lists).
- You push your own needs aside because they need you more.
- You keep investing in them – even when part of you knows you're doing too much, that it's not healthy.

What can you do?

1. Check your investment in your partner.
Carry out an inventory of your time. How much time are you spending on your partner and their issues? Are you investing more heavily in them than in yourself? Sometimes, our best efforts at support can mean we're enabling another person to stay stuck in a bad place or unhealthy habits – by doing so, we're actually disempowering them. Check you're not fostering a co-dependent relationship. Make sure you're giving them space and opportunities to take responsibility for themselves.

2. Gauge your own emotional health.
Is your own health starting to suffer? Has your anxiety increased regarding your partner? Does the relationship make you feel exhausted? Stressed or run down? Struggling to have fun? Do you worry excessively about your partner or relationship? Do you find yourself wondering if your partner's difficulties will ever end? Be honest about whether your own health is being affected –

it's a key warning sign that the relationship isn't a healthy or equitable one.

3. Get an outside viewpoint.
Being involved with someone who has high needs or depends heavily on you can cause you to lose perspective. Your thinking becomes centred around them – you can't see the situation accurately. You can't see your partner's behaviour – or personality – for what it really is. Check in with someone you trust – and listen to their advice.

4. Ask why you are persisting with this person.
Sorry, but 'because I love them' isn't a full-enough answer. Unfortunately, love does not conquer all. Clinging to that belief, even when your relationship is unhealthy, is a trap. *Love always needs to be infused with a heavy dose of realism.*

Sometimes, the reason we become 'rescuers' is rooted in our own old wounds, such as neglectful or authoritarian parenting: always having to strive for love and attention, be/do better, or desperately needing to please others. Old beliefs develop from our history and are nothing to be ashamed of, but they do need to be understood because they govern our relationship choices, thinking and behaviour.

5. Name your dreams for yourself.
Do you have your own hopes and dreams (beyond those you have with your partner)? Are you still pursuing them? Do you still see your own friends and keep up with your own interests? When you take the 'rescuer' role, all your personal plans can be sucked into the void of your partner which, eventually, will leave you hollow and empty.

6. What's good for you?

True courage lies in recognising the signs and making changes where you need to. Sometimes, this may mean ending a relationship. It's hard to leave an unhealthy partnership – it can take years to work through the complexities of it and/or summon the emotional strength to let go. But allow yourself to think about what's good for you – and hold fast to it. Eventually, it will help you break free.

Enabling (or helping your partner to hurt you)

Are you an 'enabler' in your relationship? Do you allow/support your partner's bad or destructive habits? Honestly, it's a tough question to ask. It's an even tougher one to put your hand up and confess to enabling. No-one wants to think they're a key player in another's dysfunction.

It's a good question to think about – by yourself, with no-one around to cast judgement. Because enabling will not only fail to help them – it will set you up for misery in love.

Enabling: What does it mean?

The term enabling is generally used in the context of alcohol, drugs and addiction. The most common example is when an addict's family members excuse, justify, gloss over, deny or ignore the problem. In doing so, they're shielding the addict from the full consequences of their behaviour, which gives them a leave pass to keep going.

Enabling can also refer to patterns in close relationships where one person (often unintentionally) supports problematic behaviour (or even makes it easier) to continue. Like with addiction, it commonly shows up in chronic physical/mental health issues, or money or gambling problems.

Enablers can be parents, partners, exes, friends or adult children. It's a difficult place to be. When you love someone who's out of control in some way, you can find yourself taking more responsibility for their behaviour than they're taking themselves. Even when you can't stand what your loved one is doing, you're even more scared of the consequences.

In intimate relationships, enabling tips the power balance, placing the enabler in a caregiving role that leads to exhaustion, resentment, fear and guilt; ultimately, it will erode the enabler's own health and wellbeing.

Here are some examples from enabling partners:

- If I can just get him through (this crisis), maybe he'll come to his senses.
- If I book all her medical and therapy appointments, it'll be easier for her to get help.
- I hate the 3 am calls. But if I go pick him up, at least I know he's safe.
- If I leave her, I don't know what will happen to her. I'm scared she'll hurt herself.

What can you do?

Just as a pattern of enabling takes a while to bed in, it can take a while to break. Beyond seeking professional help, which you BOTH may need, here's a place to start.

1. Show yourself some compassion.

Have you begun to organise your life and choices around your partner? Do you find yourself in a constant state of anxiety about what they'll do next? Do you rush to 'fix' or 'solve' problems, and worry about what will happen if you don't? Do you fear the next phone call or text? Or stress about what they'll be like when you walk in the door?

If you're answering 'yes' to any or all of the above, be compassionate with yourself. You may have slipped into a dysfunctional pattern – but it's coming from a place of love.

2. Be honest about your feelings.

Is it love? Or is it more like a combination of exhaustion, frustration, resentment, fear and guilt? If so, can you go on this way?

Enabling is not sustainable long term. You have to ask if what you're doing is starting to hurt you – physically, mentally and/or emotionally. Because if you keep doing what you're doing, well, you know where it's going.

3. Look at the problem from a different angle.

I know you're trying to help but ... aiding someone to continue their problematic behaviour isn't helping them. It's giving them an out clause. It's also stripping them of power. Consider how you can play things better – for their sake, as well as yours. Handing them responsibility for their behaviour and life is love, too.

4. Listen – but don't fix.

When there's a problem, don't rush to fix it or shower them with possible solutions. Allow them to come up with their own ideas. Then, when they have a good one AND follow through on it, validate them.

5. Set (little) boundaries.

All healthy relationships need boundaries. Partners need to know what's okay with you and what's not – physically, sexually and emotionally. When you get into a pattern of enabling, you let your boundaries go. They need to be re-established. When you're used to operating a particular way, however, it can be hard – and stressful. So start small. *Please don't call/text me at work unless it's an emergency. I'm only going to check my mobile phone at 5 pm for your messages. Here are some names of therapists for you to choose from and book an appointment. I won't top up your bank account when you've overspent on non-essentials.*

***

If you recognise yourself as an enabler, don't go rushing down the self-blame route: that's not productive. Instead, consider this. Your partner's behaviour has led you into enabling, and you're here because you love them and want to do the right thing. However, you need to step back and hand them back some power over their own life and future. You also need to take back some power for yourself. Being a Good Partner is about being responsible for yourself and the life YOU want to live. If you need a permission slip, here it is.

Are you as kind as you think you are?

From feeding the homeless, to holding doors open for strangers, to baking muffins for struggling friends, to scooping rubbish off pavements, we can express our kindness in a million ways.

We can quickly undermine it, too. Kindness has a false ring when you drop money in a charity bucket, then go home and snap at your innocent partner or kids because you've had a bad day. Or say mean things about a friend behind their back. Or rip apart the TV weather presenter's appearance from the safety of your own couch (especially while wearing sweat pants).

While it's human to form opinions about the people around us, how we express them holds clues to our character.

True kindness is about who we are and how we conduct ourselves: (1) in the world, (2) with our people, and (3) with ourselves. Across all three categories, kindness offers serious benefits for our mental health.

So, if you're up for some quick-and-easy self-analysis, try this test. Give yourself a tick if you answer 'yes' for each of the questions that follow.

The kindness test

The World

- ❏ I give *money, time or energy* to charity. (Three ticks if you've done all three in the past six months.)
- ❏ I always respect the environment and animals (and my actions match this).
- ❏ I never tweet or post anonymous negative comments about ANYONE. If I'm inclined to express strong opinions, I'm prepared to put my name to all of them.
- ❏ I don't make negative remarks in person or online about someone's looks, weight, clothes, race, colour, gender, sexuality, disability or any other distinguishing feature.
- ❏ I always use 'please' and 'thank you' in person AND in emails and other written correspondence. (Take an extra tick if you consistently do this at work with people lower than you in the pecking order.)
- ❏ I'm consistently courteous to retail and waiting staff (even when I'm in a rush or not getting great service).

My People

- ❏ I did one nice, unexpected thing for my partner yesterday.
- ❏ I regularly give my partner compliments that go beyond their physical appearance.
- ❏ I generally speak to my partner in a respectful tone. When we disagree, I listen closely to their point of view, and I factor it into our argument.
- ❏ When someone important to me is talking, I focus fully on what they're saying. I (always) turn off my phone and put it out of sight.

- ❑ When a friend has success or a windfall, I'm able to celebrate for, and with, them – even if I feel a tiny bit envious.
- ❑ I often call friends just to see how they're doing.
- ❑ If/when I speak to family and friends about my troubles, I'm respectful of their time and energy. I'm aware of the toll my problems might be taking on the people around me.
- ❑ I volunteer time and support to a struggling friend.
- ❑ In the past six months, I have reached out to someone who is lonely.
- ❑ I keep boundaries around friends' needs, because I know kindness is not about being a dumping ground for someone's issues, it's about supporting them to help themselves or, if necessary, seek help.

Myself

- ❑ I consistently treat my body well. I don't fill it with junk, I eat healthily and in the right proportions, I take adequate exercise, and I get medical check-ups.
- ❑ I make time for my own needs, interests and friends.
- ❑ I show myself compassion when I need it.
- ❑ I'm not overly self-critical.
- ❑ I always speak positively about MYSELF when I'm with others.
- ❑ When I do well, I take time to celebrate and enjoy it.
- ❑ I consistently treat myself with kindness, as though I'm worthy of my place in the world.

Results

20 or more ticks To be fair, that was an aspirational (aka hard) test. So if you covered yourself in glory as a kind person, well done.

Everyone else This is the dreaded 'Could do better' category. It's hard to be consistently kind in all the ways that matter. We can all do with upping our kindness game. The benefits are there for those who do.

The (immense) value of a generous spirit

When you dip inside happy, stable relationships you'll almost never find perfect exponents of whatever 'magic' there's supposed to be. Instead, you'll find super-sized servings of tolerance, compromise and – most of all – *generosity*.

I'm not talking about the Splash-the-Cash kind of generosity. That's easy (or easy if you have some cash to splash) but it has NOTHING to do with what you're like to be with, or live with, over time.

What matters is a person's Generosity of Spirit, which you can often see right at the start of a relationship. Most of us like to think we're generous but, in case the jury's still out for you, here are the most meaningful signs we're getting it right.

You're generous with your time.
Generous-spirited partners make time for the people who matter to them – partners and kids, extended families, close friends, whoever they're mentoring at work. It's not just about doing 'cool' things, it's how the time is spent – that they're being fully present for whoever they're with. Being generous in a relationship is about prioritising your partner. You'll save your time and best energy for them, rather than offering up what's left over after work, hobbies, hanging out with friends and scrolling your phone.

You're generous with your support.
When they're struggling, you're there for them. You're listening. You're being thoughtful. You're defending them – or helping them

to see the reality of a situation. They can count on you 100 per cent to have their back.

You're generous with the differences between the two of you (also known as tolerance).
I recall working with a man who was struggling in his relationship because he wanted his wife to be more like him: more outgoing, inquisitive, driven, and up for debating intellectual and political issues. No prizes for guessing that the pressure he put on her to be like this slowly destroyed their marriage. She was a lovely person, but in different ways from him. No matter how much in love you are, your partner is – and should be – different from you. If you don't enjoy (or at least accept) your differences, you're in trouble.

You're generous with your energy.
You're not always located on the couch with a box of popcorn and the remote control. Okay, sometimes you are, but you're also up for sharing the load – the chores, responsibilities with the kids/pets, the life admin, the 'emotional weight' – everything the two of you have built.

You're generous with your trust.
There is no greater, more freeing, feeling than being able to fully trust someone. Except perhaps, to have them trust you.

You're generous with others.
This doesn't mean you neglect your partner in favour of other people. It means you treat all people with respect, including those who can't improve your social status or help you get a better job. You offer your time, energy and expertise freely when you can, AND you're innately good-humoured about it.

You're generous with THEIR dreams.

You encourage and support their unique, or quirky, interests – even if you don't have a blind bit of interest in those interests.

Even if you have big plans and dreams of your own, you make space for theirs. You don't belittle their ideas or pour iced water on their endeavours. You help them to go after what makes them feel happy or content.

Of course, relationships don't run in one direction. Those that do are bound to fail. So, after you've put yourself under the grill, there's one question left. *Am I being treated with kindness, too?*

Seven-day nurturing goodwill challenge

This exercise is designed to nurture goodwill. I used to just ask people to be 'as kind as possible' to their partners for a week (as in the case described earlier), but that wasn't as effective for building goodwill as giving them specific tasks. You can train yourself to think positively about each other, but it does take practice. This exercise is useful because you can do it together, or you can just do it quietly on your own as a way of checking in on your relationship satisfaction.

Monday

Thought: *My partner is my friend.*

Action: Think of one great quality in your partner, which you also appreciate in one of your close friends. Remind yourself that it's a big reason you're together.

Tuesday

Thought: *We are a team in this relationship.*

Action: Identify one shared short-term goal you are equally invested in and are working towards together.

Wednesday

Thought: *I look forward to hanging out with my partner.*

Task: Plan a small activity/or event you can do together, even if it's just the two of you at home.

Thursday

Thought: *We share a view of the future.*

Action: Talk to your partner about what you'd like to do in the next phase of your time/life together. Write down some long-term shared goals.

Friday

Thought: *I'm physically attracted to my partner.*

Action: Think about which physical attribute you most like about your partner and use it to compliment them.

Saturday

Thought: *I'm proud of my partner.*

Action: Write down two or three sentences describing why you feel proud of your partner, including specific examples. Then tell them why.

Sunday

Thought: *I am a fantastic partner.*

Action: Do one nice, unexpected thing for your partner without expecting anything in return.

Kindness: Quick takeaways

- Charity really does begin at home.
- Turning towards your partner is better than turning away from them, and way better than turning against them.
- Kindness is the simple secret of happy relationships.
- Too much of a good thing is actually a bad thing.
- You should know what YOU bring to the relationship.
- Adoring your partner is great – but not at the expense of yourself.
- Nurturing goodwill takes effort and practice.
- Everyone deserves respect and kindness. Even (and especially) you.

PART III

WHAT'S LOVE, ACTUALLY?

A crazy little thing called love

'Love is a four-letter word spelled T-I-M-E.'
– Clinical psychologist and Holocaust survivor Dr Edith Eger

Freya is up for committing to her partner, Quinn. 'As ready as I'll ever be,' she says.

If you recall, Freya made her entrance at the start of this book. She was in love with Quinn – who she described as the ideal partner – but had found herself looking for reasons to exit the relationship.

She was picking fights and alternating between being needy and cold, almost in the hope he would leave her, so she could be the victim and not have the ongoing pressure of commitment. Also, she admitted, she could then tell herself he was rejecting her behaviour, rather than her persona, which hurt less.

The reasons were buried in her past – in her history of loss and trauma – which had caused her to become terrified of getting close to anyone, and taking an emotional risk with Quinn.

After exploring her history, what a healthy relationship looked like (to her), and what her version of being a good partner meant, she was ready to try. She was still a little apprehensive, but she knew that all love carries risk – and she was up for it.

'Well, that's it,' she says, preparing to leave our session for the last time. 'I wish you could wave a magic wand and tell me it was all going to be okay.'

I grinned. I do have a wand, purple with a star on top, given to me by one of my early supervisors, who had a rare ability to remain playful, even on the toughest days. I keep it my drawer for luck, but never take it out – partly because I want to appear sane, but also because I know too well it takes a lot more than fairy dust to make a relationship work.

As Freya stood there, I found myself scrambling for words. In parting, I wanted to say something wise. But how do you summarise the kind of investment a long-term relationship takes? What love means? What it takes?

I couldn't look her in the eye and say it'd be easy. I couldn't tell her how a relationship starts out is a reliable predictor of where it will end up. I couldn't tell her that she wouldn't face problems with Quinn, possibly big ones.

I couldn't tell her he wouldn't change, because he would, and so would she.

I couldn't tell her they would make it because – even with their best intentions – who knew what life would throw at them?

I told myself that when she left, I'd sit down and write a summary of our work, which she could take into her own journey. Those notes turned into the seven pillars and, ultimately, became this book. But all that didn't solve the dilemma of what to say in that moment.

'Love's a skill, Freya,' I finally said. 'There's no great secret. It takes time and effort to get good at it.'

***

So that's it. You've read the book; you've explored the seven pillars; you've taken the tests, tried the tools and tips, and discarded things that don't resonate with you. Most of all – and wherever you are on your relationship journey – I hope you now know more about who you are in relationships, and that you're doing what you can to be your unique version of a Good Partner.

There's no one route to love – or to getting it right – and you should run from anyone who claims they have all the answers, especially if they want your money. The only thing we know for sure is that loving someone means taking a risk. Beyond that, all you can do is be in it with both feet, do your best, and allow yourself time to grow into the role.

Many people believe that love is a choice. That we need to wake up every day, actively choose to love the one we're with, and act in ways that support our choice. It's a solid theory. But neither reality nor love will make it that easy for us. Nor will our partners.

What if we wake up filled with good intentions, our hair sticking up and with morning breath, and the person on the other side of the bed doesn't make the same choice to love us? What if they're in a bad mood, or hating their boss, or their mother's demands are driving them crazy? What if their traumatic history means they'll struggle to fully love anyone? What if they're secretly plotting to love someone else? What if life is so stressed that no-one has time to sit around, making considered choices about anything – including love?

So love is less a choice, and more a skill. A skill we can learn and develop. True, the lessons don't always come easily; love can stumble, crack or even end badly. But it can also bloom where and when we don't expect it, and rejuvenate when we've almost given up. It's a skill that, if we're willing, we can build on, from wherever we are and wherever we land.

Undoubtedly, life would be simpler without relationships, and the wounds, anxiety and conflict that often goes with them. But we still feel compelled to try. That's because love is tonic for the human spirit. It lifts us up and keeps us going; it shapes our places in the world. Research professor George Vaillant ended the renowned longitudinal Grant Study (Harvard Medical School) with: 'Happiness is Love. Fullstop.' While this 75-year study was limited in that it surveyed only men, its key message holds up. Love – not just for partners but in *all* its incarnations – quietly trumps all the other contributors to happiness. It's why we don't have our job titles, side hustles, income, successes or failures etched on our gravestones. It's the reason people miss us when we're gone.

In New Zealand, we have a Maōri proverb that goes like this:

He aha te mea nui o te ao? Maku e ki atu, he tangata, he tangata, he tangata.

It means: 'What is the most important thing in the world? It is the people, the people, the people.'

It recognises that people are the heartbeat of everything. The people we love. The people who hold us steady. The people who give us meaning. It's beautiful in its simplicity – and its truth.

What being 'in love' (really) means

I always reach for the tissues at weddings.

Even if I don't know the couple particularly well. Even if it's a TV wedding, the people getting married are actors, it's a match destined for disaster, and I'm at home on my couch.

I'm not sure why I cry at weddings, when I'm so good at regulating my emotions in front of clients. I like to think they're happy tears, which celebrate the joy of the occasion. And for the courage of those two people, who are up for giving the Big Gig a shot. But perhaps it's also because the therapist in me knows what this commitment involves – and what may lie ahead for them.

Falling in love is exciting, but it's the start of the journey, that's all. It flags almost nothing about how that love might play out. Which means it's also highly deceptive. As philosopher and author Alain de Botton reminds us: 'We seem normal only to those who don't know us very well. In a wiser, more self-aware society than our own, a standard question on any early dinner date would be: "And how are you crazy?"'

It's a great question, but we don't ask it. Instead, we get caught in a rush of emotions and hormones. We're overwhelmed with the joy (or perhaps relief) of finding someone who 'gets' us; we fix on all their 'good bits', and close our ears to any clanging warning bells. All too often, we're drawn to what feels familiar. Without being fully aware of it, we're looking to re-create love as we knew it in childhood, rather than what might be good – and healthy – for us.

We certainly don't ask about their 'crazy': the buried complexities; their core belief systems; the (often) dysfunctional ties that bind; their fear-based triggers; their negative, recurring thoughts; or what will wake them screaming in the night. Which we probably should.

Maybe, however, that would take away all the fun. And, at the outset, we need fun. Because lust and infatuation wear off, as does novelty. Desire changes, and so does sex. Real or mature love can't survive in a cauldron of emotion. It needs time to incubate, grow and develop; it needs tolerance, acceptance and forgiveness; and most of all, it needs to stand strong against the ordinary (and sometimes overwhelming) stresses of life. Love is much, much better at that than lust.

When relationships run into trouble, therapists often hear the line: 'I love my partner, but I'm not in love with them.' The first time I heard it, I was puzzled. How does anyone know when they've crossed the line, when they've officially fallen 'out' of love?

It didn't take long to figure it out, however. This phrase is often code for 'I want to have sex with someone else.' And that someone else is already hovering behind the curtain. I've heard this pitch a number of times – from both men and women. It seems to take someone else appearing in their lives for them to define their concept of 'being in love'. Which is often about sex. Fair point, but I've also seen a number of people abandon their solid (if somewhat dull) relationships for the lure of hot sex, only to find they'd leapt into a firestorm and it wasn't worth the burn.

In talking relationships with people over a long time, I've come to know that 'being in love' looks pretty much like plain old love itself.

Here's my take on the key signs of love.

You're great friends.
There's no such thing as total compatibility. Being a good partner is not about being the same as your mate, but how easily and warmly you can navigate the differences. Happy couples are genuinely close friends. You have someone you want to download the events of the day to. And who wants to listen to them. You share a laugh, and you're there for each other on the bad days as well as the good. You respect each other as people. Yes, you may have squabbles and disagreements and rough patches, but there's no-one else you'd rather come home to.

You're open-hearted with each other.
You show each other compassion. You can spill your innermost thoughts and feelings to your partner. Okay, not all of them, all the time – that might be exhausting and dull for everyone. But you can be vulnerable – physically, sexually and emotionally. And you provide a safe space for your partner to do the same with you.

You're both able to let love in.
Ideally, you both give and receive love in equal parts, but life (and relationships) isn't always a fair and equitable deal.

Interestingly, giving love is often the easier side of it. It can be difficult to open yourself up to receiving love – especially if you've been hurt. Some people are naturally good at letting love in, but most of us are a work in progress. Learning to drop your guard is worth the time and effort – it will enrich your relationships and, more broadly, your life.

Some people are incapable of loving, due to their difficult histories and life experiences. This doesn't need to be a deal-breaker – people can learn to love if they truly value someone and are willing to try. But if they're not up for trying, it will lead only to heartbreak. To love someone is to give them life's greatest gift – you have every right to expect the same in return.

You share lots of things.

Sharing your time, chores, money, parenting, possessions and/or (some) interests/activities is important. The flipside is that if you don't share, you're in trouble. One-sided relationships breed hurt and resentment. So does selfishness. So does extreme independence.

Shared experiences are vital; they're fun or uniquely challenging when you're young and – if you go the distance – they're the ones that make you smile when you're rocking out on the rest-home porch.

You're generous with each other's annoyingness.

People are confusing cocktails of good, bad and, sometimes, awful. We're all annoying. We all have bad days, get stressed and behave poorly. The success of a relationship often rests with how generously you each interpret each other's flaws, vulnerabilities, deeply embedded weirdness and just plain annoyingness. How well you can tolerate or forgive or even just let things go. With your own behaviour, it's how hard you try to curtail the worst of you for the sake of your partner.

You're affectionate, physically and emotionally.
Anyone who's been in a relationship for a long time knows sex fades. Or changes. Even with someone you left the last person for. Just saying.

Genuine affection comes in all sorts of packages, from great sex to cuddling on the couch to a tender touch on the arm to helping your partner onto her walker. As one grinning 80-something-year-old woman in a new relationship with an 80-something-year-old man put it: 'Sex is off the table for us. But I never thought I'd feel so much affection and companionship at my age. We love each other – and we're very lucky.'

The most overlooked, underrated sign of a great relationship
Although relationships are seen as a fount of happiness, they also have a reputation for being hard work. It can seem like particularly hard work when you're going through a rough patch with your partner, or you've had your heart torn to shreds.

While it's true that all relationships have their challenges, it can skew your thinking. You can end up thinking that being in a relationship is tougher than racing Bear Grylls up a mountain.

But a young man I worked with reminded me of this sign of a great relationship, which is often overlooked and definitely underrated. I thought his story was worth sharing.

When we met, he was trying to recover from a toxic relationship. He described his ex as needy, manipulative and wildly unpredictable in her moods. He'd finally broken away, but it had left him anxious and low in confidence. It wasn't the first time either; he said all his relationships had been hard – unpredictable and confusing.

He was up for giving up, forgetting about women and just hanging out with his mates. And he did – for nearly two years.

Then he met someone. When we caught up again, they'd been together six months and he was still shaking his head at his luck in finding her.

'What's so different about this relationship?' I asked.

'It's just so easy,' he said.

My client made a great point. Having an 'easy' relationship is frequently underrated because it might not seem edgy or sparky enough. Relationships are supposed to be hard ... aren't they?

No. Relationships do take effort – you can't afford to be lazy or complacent with them. And every relationship faces tests over time. However, you shouldn't wake up every day feeling like it's all 'hard slog', like you're going to work on a construction site (even if you are). Some of the best relationships work (and keep working) because of the ease both partners feel in the other's company.

Here are the key signs you might be on to a good 'easy' thing. They double as a summary for much of this book.

You feel okay about yourself – consistently.

Your partner likes you – the whole package – and tells you so. You like who you are when you're with your partner. This means you like yourself more when you're on your own or with your friends.

You feel safe without thinking about it.

This obviously means safe physically, sexually and emotionally. You're not scared when you fight. You're not scared when your partner is out, or away without you. And you feel safe to raise the 'big' topics, knowing that your partner will listen, and their reactions will be fair and reasonable, even if they don't always agree with you.

You can go for hours without talking.

You're as comfortable in silence as you are with talking. This means you feel fully relaxed around them, which is a wonderful thing.

You know who's walking through the door.
You don't wait nervously to see which version of your partner has shown up for your anxiety to settle. You're always happy to see them *before* they show up – as well as when they do.

You sort out disagreements quickly.
You both own your mistakes and apologise when necessary. You don't hold grudges, storm out, give the silent treatment, use sex as a weapon or any other dysfunctional 'battle' strategies.

Your partner encourages you to see your friends.
Wow. Your partner wants you to have a life beyond them. This makes you want them to have one, too.

You like hanging out together.
You don't have to spend every waking minute together but, because you genuinely enjoy your partner's company, you create time for it. You both initiate things for the two of you to do and, shock-horror, you have fun.

You look for the gold in each other.
You orient to the positives. You accept your partner for who they are, as they are. The fact that they annoy you sometimes doesn't matter. Or not too much, at least. But your capacity to tolerate, forgive and love them in spite of it, however, does.

It just feels good.
You struggle to put it into words, but your relationship just feels good. And you feel good. As blind and deaf American author Helen Keller said, 'the best and most beautiful things in the world cannot be seen or even heard, but must be felt with the heart.'

Beyond couples: Other ways to love

A young woman I 'met' on Zoom during a COVID-19 lockdown was struggling with being on her own.

In her early 30s, she'd been focused on her career so had never had a serious partner. It had never bothered her until the isolation and loneliness of lockdown brought it home.

'Everything you ever read tells you that human connection is vital to happiness,' she said. 'If I don't have a partner, and if I don't find someone, how can I ever be happy?'

I could see how she'd joined the dots. Plenty of research positively correlates human connection with life satisfaction and reminds us of the dark side of loneliness. She'd equated this with having a partner because, as she said, society is largely set up for couples. Everything from hotel rooms to travel deals to turning up at parties plugs the notion that 'two is better than one.' But two is not better than one, at all. You only have to witness a distressed couple, or watch a marriage unravel in bitterness, to know that a fulfilled single life is way better – and healthier – than a miserable co-joined one. Not only that, but life can be easier when you only have to consider yourself.

Having a partner is great if – and only if – you have a good one. (And *you* are a good one, too.) There are many ways to love, to bring feelings of warmth and love into your life. A broader, higher aim than being someone's partner is to be a loving person.

Ancient Greek philosophers advocated for this broader view of love by breaking it into four parts. The idea is you don't have to demonstrate all four kinds of love all the time to be a loving person. I love this concept because people who aren't in relationships shouldn't have to feel second best in love. And those in miserable relationships shouldn't have to feel they're not loving people either.

- **Eros:** Romantic love, the intimate/sexual love you have for another person.
- **Storge:** An empathy bond, refers to affection in families or within close groups.
- **Philia:** The bond between friends. Philia also includes love for the self.
- **Agape:** Love for humanity and spiritual/religious forms of love.

While the concept of *philia* covers the love you have for yourself, I believe self-love or acceptance needs a category all of its own. Maybe that's because, as a therapist, I have come to know how much self-love – even a little self-compassion – can buoy people. If you allow it to, feeling good about yourself will sustain you all the days of your life.

So, with respect to the ancient Greeks, here's a big-picture view of love followed by some extra tips for nurturing the longest relationship you'll ever have – the one you have with yourself.

How to be a loving person

Treat yourself well first.
Loving people understand the importance of treating themselves well. They put time and energy into it – without guilt.

I'm careful about introducing the concept of self-love to clients, even though most people concede it's a good idea. You have to tread lightly with self-love, and you have to do it in a way that matches the person in front of you. If I was to tell someone to stand naked in the mirror, chanting affirmations about how much they adore themselves, I'd probably never see them again.

So it's easier – and lower risk – to talk to clients about how they could treat themselves well, or better. Some will choose massages, exercise, long walks or eating better. Others will aim to stop themselves every time they begin to mutter a critical or self-defeating word. It doesn't matter where you start or what you do, as long as it points in the right direction.

Make regular deposits in family and friendship banks.

People who do this show love consistently with their words and behaviour towards those who matter to them. They don't have important conversations on the run. They sit still and listen. They give their time, energy and support freely. They text, call or check in for no good reason. They do favours for others when they're not being paid for it – and without expecting payback. In summary, they deposit more than they withdraw.

Allow love to flow to you.

Loving people are receivers – as well as givers – of love. It sounds obvious but, for a lot of people, receiving love or intimacy is surprisingly hard. Actually, it's not that surprising, when you peer into histories and traumatic events that have made them afraid to love. Or afraid to love fully. Or do weird things when they think someone else loves them. Perhaps they're scared of loss, abandonment or rejection? Perhaps they just don't know how.

While letting love in comes more easily to some than others, we can all keep developing our skills. The key step is to accept that all worthwhile love carries risk – we shouldn't run from it without reason.

Arrive at a place of forgiveness.

Look, forgiveness is hard. It's a nice idea, until you try to do it. Just when you think you've made peace with someone from your past, something will trigger you and you'll be back in that dark place, ruminating, seething, and feeling hurt and sad.

Forgiveness is for saints. All power to them. For the rest of us, it's about accepting what happened then loosening our grip on it, so it doesn't have the power to control, or even manipulate, the rest of our lives.

Have compassion for humanity.

Loving people do 'big picture' love, which stretches beyond self, family and close loved ones to all of humanity. And they'll maintain it consistently. This can be hard to do – and extremely difficult to keep up – because we all get lost in our own stress and worry at times. But loving people keep their eyes up; their love shines out in the world, too.

***

If you can say yes to those things, congratulations. Considering yourself as a loving person is your foundation for love. Now, it's time to talk about the most important person in your world, the only relationship you can be sure of improving – and the one most central to shaping your life.

The only person who'll never leave you

Theory suggests that, before we can fully love someone else, we need to love ourselves. No, we don't. We can love another and still dislike ourselves. I've seen it a thousand times over in the therapy room. I have the evidence.

Love is better when we like and trust ourselves, because we can relax and enjoy it. We don't feel so desperate in love. We don't cling to it. We know that, if love is not there, we're okay in our own company.

You don't have to love yourself from the outset, but you should work on having some sort of relationship with yourself. If you don't, it's like going on a very bad date that never ends. Like it or not, you're going the distance with this person, so you might as well be friends.

For many of us, friendship is an easier pill to swallow than self-love because everyone can do friendship in one way or another. It means treating yourself kindly, as you would a great mate. It's easier to treat yourself well, than love yourself well.

A Quick Guide to Self-Friendship

Date yourself.
Not all the time and exclusively – that might be weird. But learn to hang out with yourself, and go out alone. It'll build your confidence as well as give you space for your own ideas. Watch your creativity go up a notch.

Dress up.
This doesn't mean you have to throw out the trackpants. But dress up, or wear your favourite clothes, as often as you can. Knowing and feeling you look good breeds confidence.

Know your strengths.
Keep a list of your best qualities in your phone to use as a pick-me-up when you're feeling low. If you don't know what they are, ask your people to help.

When you know your strengths, it's easier to spot evidence of them. Every time you play to them, give yourself some praise.

My best three qualities are:

* ....
* ....
* ....

Move from 'to do' to 'have done'.

Instead of constantly worrying about all you haven't done, keep a log of everything you've achieved. You'll be amazed at how quickly the list builds up. It's healthy to take time to measure yourself backwards.

Give it a go before asking for help.

Give yourself time to be a problem-solver. Think and try before you ask. This promotes a feeling of self-efficacy, that you are a capable person.

Ban negative self-talk.

Or at least limit it. We all do a little of this and some do it a lot, but it NEVER helps. Catch yourself when you're doing this and say 'no'. Atone or apologise for your mistakes, then let go. Speak to (and advise) yourself as you would a close friend.

Use your body.

Not just for flaunting, adorning or sex. When people don't like their physical selves, they'll often neglect themselves. Moving your body, even if it's just a walk or stretch, helps to connect mind and body.

Clean up your space.

Pleasant environments help promote healthy internal feelings, so clean up your desk, your room, your office, your home. Your environments include the people in your world, so think about those too.

Compliment yourself daily.

Or all the time if you want to. Once a day, lock in on your finer qualities (not just the physical). This reorients you to everything that's good about you – and there's a lot.

Accept your own crazy.

This is all those little quirks that make you, you. Instead of rejecting them, or going all out to change yourself, accept that's who you are. You can make tweaks and improvements in how you roll, and you can certainly work on being a better partner, but accept the foundation of who you are. There's great freedom in that.

Necessary (and wonderful) endings

I'll leave the final word to a woman I bumped into at the local Botanic Gardens, as I was writing this chapter.

'Hey!' Dee said, swooping in for a hug. She and I had worked together a few years previously. Dee has a big, warm personality and a cackling laugh; this lifted the mood of the whole office and forced you to join in. We'd shared lunches and banter, and I'd also got to know her partner, Jonathan, a quiet steady man, who frequently picked her up from work.

She'd since retired and we'd lost touch. Today, she'd brought her grand-daughters to the park to give their mum a break. We stood chatting while the kids checked out the playground.

As we talked, I noticed how she referred to herself. She used 'I', not 'we'. I thought it was strange, or at least different. She and Jonathan were your 'peas in a pod' older couple; you rarely saw one without the other. But he'd have been in his 70s now, so it struck me that he might have died.

'How's Jon?' I finally said, bracing myself for sad news.

She paused for a second, then looked me in the eye. 'We broke up.'

I blinked. Death, I could've understood, but a breakup? They were, in my mind, the ideal couple. One of those rare couples who still liked each other after decades together, who showed you what love might be like if you could manage to go the distance. They'd raised a family together, they'd travelled widely, they'd fully supported each other's careers, and they always spoke lovingly to, and about, each other. But – apparently – it was over.

'Oh, I'm sorry to hear that,' I managed.

She smiled. 'It's okay. It was a long time coming.'

Was it? Really? There was never any hint of trouble, as far as I could remember. But I should know as well as anyone that what people present to the world is often not the truth of it.

'How are you doing, Dee?' I asked. What I was really thinking was: *How are you holding up? How are you coping without him?* I couldn't imagine she'd be happy alone, even though I believe wholeheartedly that your relationship with yourself is the most important one you'll ever have.

'I'm wonderful,' she said, touching my arm as if to reassure me. Perhaps I hadn't hidden my surprise as well as I'd thought. 'Truly.'

Shortly after that, she went back to her grandkids and, as I walked away, I heard her crazy laugh ring out across the park. I smiled at the quiet reminder she'd given me about love, life and everything.

People change. Relationships are not always what you think they are. Nor do they always land where you hope they will. And no matter what life throws at you, there are moments of wonderful everywhere – if you're willing to look for them.

Acknowledgements

Any writer knows it takes a Herculean effort to transform a bunch of ideas and thoughts into a book with a life of its own. I can claim only part of it. So, my sincere thanks to everyone who helped get *The Good Partner* to here; all contributions were gratefully received!

Special thanks to:

Publisher Alex Hedley and the wonderful team at HarperCollins*Publishers* New Zealand; Senior Editor Lachlan McLaine and his colleagues at HarperCollins*Publishers* Australia.

My clients for the stories, insights and lessons they've so generously passed on to me over the years. The laughs, too. Therapy is not all serious.

And last, but never least, to my husband Kev, my personal editor, who continues to be his own unique version of a Good Partner. Lucky me.

Other books by Karen Nimmo

My Bum Looks Brilliant in This:
The one true secret of lasting weight loss

Fish Pie is Worse Than Cancer

Fatty and Skinny
– a YA novel

Busy as F*ck:
10 on-the-couch sessions to diagnose,
explain and treat busy as f*ck people everywhere